coach yourself

IT'S YOUR
WHAT ARE
TO DO

LIFE – YOU GOING WITH IT?

coach yourself

make real changes in your life

Anthony Grant & Jane Greene

www.yourmomentum.com
the stuff that drives you

What is momentum?

Momentum is a completely new publishing philosophy, in print and online, dedicated to giving you more of the information, inspiration and drive to enhance who you are, what you do, and how you do it.

Fusing the changing forces of work, life and technology, momentum will give you the bright stuff for a brighter future and set you on the way to being all you can be.

Who needs momentum?

Momentum is for people who want to make things happen in their career and their life, who want to work at something they enjoy and that's worthy of their talent and their time.

Momentum people have values and principles, and question who they are, what they do, and who for. Wherever they work, they want to feel proud of what they do. And they are hungry for information, stimulation, ideas and answers …

Momentum online

Visit *www.yourmomentum.com* to be part of the talent community. Here you'll find a full listing of current and future books, an archive of articles by momentum authors, sample chapters and self-assessment tools. While you're there, post your worklife questions to our momentum coaches and sign up to receive free newsletters with even more stuff to drive you.

More momentum

If you need more drive for your life, try one of these titles, all published under the momentum label:

'Finally an end to the bullshit. Unsentimental, straightforward, to the point. This is the most exciting, best researched self-help book you will ever read.'

'These life coaches are direct, informative, undaunted, patient, tolerant of occasional back-slides and never condescending or simple-minded. The pages abound with helpful case examples from every age and walk of life. To boot, the text is literate, fun and energising to read. The tasks make one get out a pencil and pad to start work right now.'

Rosemary H. Balsam, M.D., Psychiatrist, Psychoanalyst, Yale University, USA

PEARSON EDUCATION LIMITED

Head Office
Edinburgh Gate
Harlow CM20 2JE
Tel: +44 (0)1279 623623
Fax: +44 (0)1279 431059

London Office:
128 Long Acre, London WC2E 9AN
Tel: +44 (0)20 7447 2000
Fax: +44 (0)20 7240 5771
Website: www.business-minds.com

First published in Great Britain in 2001

© Pearson Education Limited 2001

The right of Anthony Grant and Jane Greene to be identified as authors of this work has been asserted by them in accordance with the Copyright, Designs and Patents Act 1988.

ISBN 1843 04013 1

British Library Cataloguing in Publication Data
A CIP catalogue record for this book can be obtained from the British Library.

10 9 8 7 6 5

Typeset by Northern Phototypesetting Co. Ltd, Bolton
Printed and bound in Great Britain by Biddles Ltd, Guildford and King's Lynn

Cover design by Heat
Text design by Claire Brodmann Book Designs, Lichfield, Staffs

The Publishers' policy is to use paper manufactured from sustainable forests.

thank you…

to everyone who has helped in the preparation of this book.

Special thanks to Lennart, Leo and Stanley Petterson and Georgie, Ben and Toby Grant, for their invaluable help, support and advice.

about the authors

Jane Greene is a writer, editor and consultant specializing in management training and life-long learning. After taking a first degree in English and Philosophy she began her career as an English teacher and then after completing a masters degree in Artificial Intelligence embarked on a second career as managing editor at the Open College, London, producing multi-media, open and distance-learning packages for adults. After some time at St Bartholomew's Medical College developing interactive, computer-based training packages for medical students, she set up her own open and distance-learning consultancy. Her recent clients include London University, Unison, the Home Office, Botanic Gardens Conservation International, Pearn Kandola, the Burton Morris Consultancy, Chartered Institute of Personnel and Development, and the Open University of Spain.

Anthony Grant is a coaching psychologist. He holds a BA (Hons) (first class honours) in Psychology from the University of Sydney, Australia, and a Masters of Arts in Behavioural Science from the Department of Psychology at Macquarie University, Sydney, where he is completing his PhD. His PhD topic is 'Evidenced-based coaching for enhanced performance: the impact on metacognition, socio-cognition and goal attainment'.

Tony's background is most definitely grounded in the realities of the commercial world. Having left school at the age of 15 with no qualifications, Tony completed his training as a carpenter and ran his own contracting business. Embarking on a second career, he made a successful transition into direct sales and marketing, before beginning tertiary studies as a mature student and commencing a third career as a coaching psychologist.

In January 2000 Tony established the world's first university-based coaching psychology unit at the Department of Psychology, the University of Sydney, where he teaches and co-ordinates the world's first post-graduate degree programme in Coaching Psychology.

Tony has more than 15 years' experience in facilitating individual and organizational change, and has worked with a wide range of individuals and organizations, from primary school teachers through to the senior leadership team of the Royal Australian Air Force, and senior corporate executives. His coaching research and practice has frequently been reported in the national and international media. Tony's coaching practice and teaching emphasizes the use of empirically validated techniques and draws on the cognitive-behavioural and solution-focused approaches.

opening

coach yourself

momentum

chapter one
change happens
why is it important to be able to change?

chapter two
BYO

can you be your own life coach?

chapter three
all change
what works and what doesn't

chapter four
hopes and dreams
what do you really want?

chapter five
whatever turns you on
exploring motivation

chapter six
from negative to positive
turning ANTs into PETs

opening

coach yourself

momentum

chapter seven
solutions, solutions, solutions

chapter eight
gathering strength

chapter nine
staying on track

chapter ten
do it with a friend
co-coaching

chapter eleven
success

chapter twelve
coach yourself: a life-coaching programme for change

01

chapter one
change happens
why is it important to be able to change?

Welcoming change

'All things change; nothing abides. Into the same river one cannot step twice.'
Heraclitus, 500 BC

This book is about embracing, welcoming and inviting change into our lives. It is about finding a way to live a more purposeful, more fulfilling, more joyful life. The techniques in this book will help you to change unwanted or unhelpful behaviour and to find ways to live the life you want to live.

But we are not talking about wishful thinking or merely dreaming of a brighter life. Everything in this book works. Every technique, strategy and change process in this book has been scientifically tested and validated. If you use the techniques presented in Chapter 12 you *will* make changes – your life will improve and you will be better equipped to choose the life you want to lead.

Change is all around us

Life is change – and always has been – but now the world is changing at an unprecedented rate. Universities and business schools have whole departments devoted to change management. Organizations and corporations need to prepare to cope with change before it's even happened. But with change come both opportunity and threat.

'If we want things to stay as they are, things will have to change.'
Giuseppe di Lampedusa, *The Leopard*, 1960[1]

Competition seems to be everywhere. Everything is available to us. We have so much choice, life seems to become more and more confusing. Travel gets easier and cheaper, we can go wherever we want, be whoever we want, via the internet we can communicate with whoever we want whenever we want.

'Like it or not, change cannot be turned on and off. At the moment it is flowing uncontrollably. Put your hand over it and the water will spread in all directions. Sit back and you will drown.'

Jonas Ridderstrale, Kjell Nordstrom, *Funky Business*[2]

Choice brings conflict

But with this choice and change comes conflict. Every day the number of decisions we have to make gets bigger and bigger. Even to buy a cup of coffee now we have to choose – espresso, cappuccino, latte, decaf, full-fat milk, half-fat milk, filter. It is no longer enough just to order a coffee. We have to make decisions.

We are bombarded with information and choice.

We are bombarded with information and choice while at the same time the certainties of life are taken away. We all know that the 'job for life' is gone. Even planning our careers properly is more difficult because we don't know whether the kind of work we train for now will exist in ten, five, even one year's time. New jobs will be created. We can't train for them yet because we don't even know what they are. But we try to be ready. We must retrain, switch direction, and train again. And when we do have a job we must be prepared to undergo continuous training just to stay where we are. This is especially true for some jobs. Nurses in the UK, for example, have to agree to undertake at least 35 hours of study each year, just to remain qualified. The technology changes so fast that unless they constantly retrain they cannot hope to keep up. This is true for so many occupations nowadays. Stop for a moment and you're left behind.

So we are locked into a kind of paradox. On the one hand we have to be able to change and adapt, on the other, we want and need the kind of certainties that our grandparents' generation had. We are flailing around looking for something that is constant.

Fear of change

Many of us are afraid of change, afraid of the future. We would rather stay with what we know, with what is safe, even if it is making us unhappy.

'You can't teach an old dog new tricks.'
'Better the devil you know.'
'It'll be out of the frying pan into the fire.'

All these old adages remind us to be afraid or at least suspicious of the future and of change. The irony is that we can't stop change. Time passes, seasons change, we grow older, we can't help it. Life is change. We may think that by doing nothing things will stay as they are, but we know this is not true. Perhaps it is that fear – of things changing without our consent – that makes us cling on to jobs we don't like, relationships that we know have grown stale, or habits that don't make us happy but at least are familiar.

Change and passing time have always been difficult, and often frightening, something which human beings have tried for centuries to come to terms with.

'Time is like a river made up of the events which happen, and its current is strong: no sooner does anything appear than it is swept away, and another comes in its place and will be swept away too.'

Marcus Aurelius Antoninus, AD 121–180, *Meditations* 1v. 43

The difference now is simply the rate of change. That is what is so dizzying. We hardly have time to get used to one idea before it has gone, replaced by something else.

'I have seen so many changes during my lifetime, including two world wars. But I think the biggest change is the speed and amount that people travel. I left Boston to go to live in Paris in 1932. I travelled with my sister on board the RMS Majestic. She was the largest steam ship in the world at the time. It took us six days to reach France. Now people hop on planes to go here, there and everywhere. If I had to say what the biggest change was I'd say it was that, Tourism. It just hardly existed when I was young.'

Alice, 90, teacher, writer, mother

Alice tells this story sitting in a café in Paris. Halfway through, her mobile phone rings. It is her son calling from Mexico. Only 20 years ago this would have seemed unbelievable; in 1932, it would have been pure science fiction.

For our children, who are always way ahead of us, the changes will happen even faster. Much of what they learn today will almost certainly be outdated by the time they reach adulthood. To truly equip our children for the future the schools need to teach them how to adapt, how to solve problems and how to make sense of the world around them. These are skills they are going to need no matter what.

'My little grandson said to me the other day, "What are those things called, Grandpa, you know those glass things you use if you haven't got a mobile phone? Oh yes, I know, "phone boxes". To him they were already history.'
Jim, 67

Making changes

Children of course mostly do adapt and change to fit in with what is going on around them. But as we grow older it gets more and more difficult. Often we want to change a habit or behaviour that seems unhelpful or even damaging, yet we just can't do it. We find ourselves in the same situation again and again but we cannot find a way out. Sometimes we seek help, through a counsellor or therapist, a personal trainer, a guru, an expert of some kind or other. We spend thousands of pounds on special 'diet food' or nicotine patches or different kinds of therapies and courses. But so often, despite all this effort, the behaviour stays with us.

Trying to achieve something and failing again and again becomes dispiriting.

Trying to achieve something and failing again and again becomes dispiriting. In the end we give up.

'I was meant to be heavy.'
'I'll stop smoking at New Year.'
'I just don't like work, I'll never find a job to suit me.'

'I'm a control freak, I know I am, I can't help it.'

'I suppose I'm just lazy.'

We label ourselves and accept our limitations. Gradually, as we go through life, we give up on our dreams, settle for less than we want, or do the things other people think are right for us. It is easier, less disappointing, less hurtful to give up our dreams than to face the constant disappointment of not living up to them.

Yet some people do manage to make changes. Some people do manage to live their dreams. Some people do manage to change destructive or negative behaviour and reinvent themselves. How do they do it?

There are no easy answers, but in this book we present tools, techniques and attitudes that can help you create lasting, positive changes. If you use them you will make changes in your life. They have been proven to work.

It may not be a fashionable view but to make changes in your life takes courage. One thing is certain. If you don't try, you can't fail, but nor can you succeed.

Take action

Some people do manage to make changes in their lives. How is this? What is it that enables some people to fulfil their dreams while the rest of us sit around talking about it but doing nothing?

'In the Olympic Games it is not the most beautiful and the strongest that are crowned but those who compete (for it is some of these that are victorious), so those who act win, and rightly win, the noble and good things in life.'   Aristotle, *Ethics*

It is simply this, the will to act, that makes the difference – taking the first step and setting off in the direction we want to go, then planning very carefully the route that will lead towards a more successful, more fulfilled life.

'True life is lived when tiny changes occur.'   Leo Tolstoy

About the book

Based on scientifically validated and tested psychological techniques, this highly practical book will teach you how to make lasting, positive, inspirational change in your life. It will help you to identify goals and to reach them. You will learn how to be your own, solution-focused life coach. Life coaching empowers people to make lasting, positive, inspirational change in both their private and working lives.

How to use the book

Each chapter of this book deals with a different aspect of the Coach Yourself programme. At the end of each chapter you will find steps to follow. These refer to the steps in Chapter 12, which presents the entire programme and is designed for you to work through on your own or with a friend or colleague (*see* Chapter 10).

In an evaluation of the Coach Yourself programme at the University of Sydney, people found that they could change negative behaviour patterns that they had been struggling with for an average of three years. These included starting a new business, enhancing time-management skills, career development, and improving interpersonal skills.

The tools and techniques presented in this book will provide you with a simple but powerful way of getting and keeping your life on track.

02

chapter two
BYO

can you be your own life coach?

coach yourself

What is life coaching?

Life coaching will help you to ask yourself these three questions:

◆ What do I want to do with my life?

◆ What is stopping me from doing it?

◆ What am I going to do about it?

The questions are simple but the answers may not be. A life coach will help you to find the answers that are right for you. It's like having a personal trainer for your life and career, who will work on improving and enhancing all areas of your life. They will help you work out where you want to go and plan strategies to get you there. Life coaching uses a series of techniques and strategies that will help you to:

◆ clarify what you want from life

◆ set yourself effective goals

◆ monitor your progress on your journey of change

◆ stay focused and challenged

◆ stick to your commitments

◆ continually reassess and re-examine your ideas, plans and strategies

◆ identify your life values.

It will also help you to understand what is important in your life and what fulfilment is for you. Increasingly people are turning to life coaches to help them organize their lives.

'Some identify happiness with virtue, some with practical wisdom, others with a kind of philosophic wisdom, others with these or one of these, accompanied by pleasure.' Aristotle, *Ethics*

Where has coaching come from?

During the 1960s the business world started to look at sports coaching and adapt the techniques for use in training and development. These techniques have been developed and enhanced and today coaching is one of the fastest-growing personal development strategies used by chief executive officers (CEOs), entrepreneurs, professionals, people in the midst of a career change and others struggling with life issues.

Instead of running faster, jumping higher, scoring more goals or winning more matches, life coaches work with their clients on issues such as:

◆ work/life balance

◆ dealing with conflict

◆ increasing productivity

◆ effective leadership

◆ working as part of a team

◆ communication skills

◆ relationships

◆ parenting skills.

Life coaching has its roots in:

◆ sports coaching

◆ business consulting and management training

◆ education

◆ clinical and counselling psychology.

Life coaching borrows from all these disciplines, but there are important differences.

The sporting model

No serious sportsman or woman would expect to get very far in their chosen sport without a coach. To succeed, athletes need someone who can guide them towards their personal best. The challenges of sport are physical, mental and technical. To play sport you need to have at least:

◆ a level of fitness

◆ a good mental attitude, including drive and determination

◆ a level of skill and mastery over yourself and your equipment.

In addition to developing technical expertise, sports coaches help their clients to:

◆ set performance targets

◆ cope with pressure and stress

◆ develop and maintain vision

◆ deal with negative beliefs that might affect performance

◆ maintain motivation

◆ analyze performance

◆ stay focused.

Sport crosses all boundaries, including, age, gender, race, religion, social standing, education. Everyone can take part in sport. The rules and goals are well defined. Each sport has its own system of rules and regulations. To judge how well an individual or team is doing, just look at the scoreboard or stopwatch.

In sport each person can set their own standard.

In sport each person can set their own standard. If you run a marathon you can aim to win or you can aim just to complete the course. Success depends on the goals you set yourself. Sport offers a lot of opportunity to strive, to succeed and to win, whatever that means for you.

It is perhaps this very individual nature of sports coaching that is now appealing to a wider audience. As the world becomes more complex, so you have to work harder to find your own way, to determine what success means to you. There is no easy formula for success because success is different for each individual. A life coach is someone who is on your side, working with you to help you to set and reach your personal goals.

Coaching and therapy

Coaching is not psychotherapy but it does use techniques derived from clinical psychology. The main differences between coaching and therapy are:

◆ coaching deals with clients who are basically functional, albeit dissatisfied with some aspect of their lives. So people may come to coaching for a variety of reasons, but not necessarily because they have a problem. It may simply be that, like an athlete, they want to improve their performance in a particular area of their life

◆ the emphasis in coaching is less on unravelling and understanding problems and difficulties, and more on focusing on finding solutions. It is very future oriented

◆ coaching does not deal with clinical issues, such as depression or high levels of anxiety; for these you need to see your doctor.

Coaching and training

Coaching also owes a debt to training techniques and philosophies, but there are major differences. Training is about teaching particular skills, and the agenda for any training programme is set by the organization or the trainer. In coaching practice, it is the client who sets the agenda and determines the goals to be achieved. Coaching looks at a wide range of life issues, including the skills you might need to get on in your job or your home life.

Coaching and mentoring

A mentor is usually an expert in a particular field. They will work within that field to help more junior practitioners gain knowledge, skills and experience. A life coach is not necessarily an expert in the field of influence of the client. Rather they will work with the client to identify and reach significant targets and goals.

Basic notions

There are some basic notions behind coaching techniques:

◆ People are essentially able.

◆ You know yourself best so accept your own definition of your situation.

◆ Acknowledge and take the credit for your successes.

◆ Focus on the solution, not the problem.

◆ A problem is something that you have, not are.

Who uses coaching?

Coaching is used increasingly in the business world. Management coaches work with their clients to, for example:

◆ enhance their effectiveness in their present job

◆ develop specific skills

◆ plan and implement a career path

◆ manage stress, work/life balance, clarify personal values.

Corporations are finding that coaching is good both for organizations and employees. A survey[1] of more than 4,000 corporations revealed that corporate coaching improves the performance of individuals, leads to better client service, raises confidence, improves relationships at work, develops people for the next level and increases goal achievement. These benefits lead to increased profits and competitiveness for the company and better employee retention.

Companies are increasingly turning to coaching techniques to develop employees they want to retain.

'In the '70s and '80s, "coaching" was usually a euphemism for helping problem employees. Today most human resource (HR) professionals understand coaching as a focused, one-on-one process intended to maximize management and leadership potential or behaviour change in the workplace.'

Andrea Huff, senior vice-president of San Francisco-based Lee Hecht Harrison, an international outplacement and career services firm[2]

Why is coaching necessary?

People and organizations are turning to coaching because the world is changing, and fast. Businesses must keep reinventing themselves if they are to survive and people must keep reinventing themselves and updating their skills in all areas of their lives if they are to be employed by these businesses. In a world where so much is available to us we have to learn how to make choices and to choose the life path that will serve us best. This means working out what our values are, what is important to us and what we want to spend our time and energy doing.

There are two sides to the equation.

Modern organizations want and need outstanding performers.

Modern organizations want and need outstanding performers if they are to succeed. But the outstanding performers do not want to stay in one organization if they are not learning and developing. So companies have to provide their employees with opportunities to learn and develop and need to offer them challenges and stimulation. At the same time downsizing means that one person may have to take on the jobs and responsibilities that were previously covered by a whole team or department. Only highly trained and motivated people will be able to cope with the pressure and stress this causes. Companies need to offer their employees techniques and strategies to concentrate their energies and efforts in the most efficient and effective way. There is no longer any slack. Organizations cannot afford to have people who are not being used effectively or who do not feel stimulated and excited by what they do.

'In the post-war years, planning and control systems were the tools that enabled companies to grow and helped managers deal with sprawling enterprises. Yet many of the problems companies experience today are inherent in the strategy–structure–systems doctrine that produces these tools. The systems that allowed managers to control employees also inhibited creativity and initiative. Today the challenge for top-level managers is to engage the knowledge and skills of each person in the organisation in order to create what the authors call an individualised corporation.'

Changing the role of top management – beyond systems to people[3]

Where have the techniques in this book come from?

The Coaching Psychology unit at the department of psychology at the University of Sydney runs the world's first (and at present only) postgraduate course in coaching psychology that specifically trains psychologists and human resource practitioners who want to work as coaches. The coaching theories, tools and techniques in this book have been developed at the Coaching Psychology unit and are all evidence based. This means that in clinical trials they have been shown to be effective.

What is a clinical trial?

In a clinical trial a group of people are randomly allocated to either a treatment group or a control group and a number of factors are measured before and after the treatment programme. In the case of coaching these factors could be goal attainment, anxiety, stress or depression, and ability to set and achieve goals. If the coaching or the treatment programme really does work, there should be a significant difference between the group that undergoes the programme and the group that doesn't.

All the techniques in this book are:

◆ driven by psychological theory

◆ based on scientific evidence.

Coaching is about change

Some people can decide to make a change in their life and move directly to their goal in the quickest possible manner, with no deviation or hesitation. Some people are really good at *starting* to make changes but their change programme seems to grind to a halt very quickly. Others are really good at starting out and can maintain progress for a while, but always seem to come up against blocks. Often it seems that no matter what we do, we just can't break through these blocks. Each time we try to enact a change programme and are defeated by the same (or similar) blocks, we feel less and less capable of creating the changes we want. Over time, not surprisingly, we start to expect failure and increasingly doubt our ability to get what we want out of life. We settle for second or even third best. This book will help you to put into place a successful programme for real change. If you use the techniques, they will work.

Overview of the coaching process

Most people come to coaching with some level of dissatisfaction, something in their lives they want to change. Perhaps you have unfulfilled dreams, something you wish you had done but haven't managed to achieve so far. Perhaps you are aware of missed opportunities in your life, a chance that you didn't take, a lead you didn't follow up, an invitation to do something that in retrospect seems like an interesting move.

'I was offered a job in America when I was 17. I almost went but in the end I said no. I've always wondered how my life would have turned out if I'd said yes instead.' Sven, 56, shipbuilder, Sweden

Sometimes the decision to make a change is precipitated by some personal crisis, or change. Good events as well as bad can rock our view of the world and prompt us to reassess what we are doing and where we are going. But often it is just that we feel we need to move on, to change something in our lives that is causing us problems. Whether you come to coaching as part of your response to a specific crisis or whether you have simply experienced a growing feeling of discontent, in order to make real changes in your life you need a vision of where you want to be.

To be useful, your vision needs to be quite broad. What we call 'fuzzy vision' (*see* Chapter 4), a general idea of the sort of direction you want to move in. It needs to be inspirational and motivational and it needs to sit well with your beliefs and values.

You probably already have a fuzzy vision of the way you want your life to be. You are almost certainly fulfilling some sort of view of the way you think life ought to go. The trouble is we so often just carry on along the road that seems to be mapped out for us without really examining whether it is what we really want. Traumatic events in our lives throw rocks under our feet and we often end up having to change direction entirely. Coaching will help you to take some time to look at your broad vision and work out if it is really what you want.

A vision is not enough. We need specific goals and plans to get us there. The best plans are flexible ones. We can't know what's going to work until we try, so we need some sort of mechanism to alter our plans if they are not leading us in the right direction. Coaching teaches us to monitor our progress and change direction when necessary. As we reach milestones on the way we need to take time to celebrate our successes. The key to it all is action, continuous and deliberate action. Without it none of this will work.

Most people are not intrinsically lazy or weak willed, but they are very busy.

Most people are not intrinsically lazy but they are very busy. We forget what it was we intended to do. We get distracted by other things. Coaching helps us to remember. It keeps us on track and helps us to make sure we are living our lives according to our beliefs and ideals.

The more we succeed, the better it feels. The exhilaration of being in control of your life is a powerful motivator. It can lead you to great things. You make the plans, you develop the skills, and it works out if you make the changes. The feeling is incredible, and not suprisingly it affects other areas of your life.

Coaching has a knock-on effect

If we can learn to take control of one area of our life and make changes necessary to keep us heading in the direction we want to be going, it seems we automatically become more effective in other areas. Research at the University of Sydney has shown that students who used coaching techniques developed at the university to improve their study skills made unexpected beneficial changes in other unrelated areas of their lives. These effects were still there one year later.

'I work for myself and I love what I do. I am always busy. My friends think I have the perfect life. The trouble is for the last four years I have been working on an emergency basis. When a job comes in I drop everything until it is done. Then when it is finished I face the next emergency. There are all sorts of jobs that I just never get round to doing. My office is chaos. Things are spilling out of the drawers. I have three desk lamps on my desk, only one of which works. Stacks of books and piles of papers are everywhere. And I don't have enough power points. I never get around to doing any filing, whether virtual or paper. I have three separate address books, each with pieces of paper falling out of them. I have so little time to spend with my wife and children. I also feel that I am becoming increasingly unfit. I eat badly and I almost never have time to exercise.

I decided I needed help. A friend recommended a life coach. I was sceptical but it was worth a try. At the first session I talked about my work problems. He made me make a list of all the things I hoped to achieve by the end of our coaching sessions.

They were: sort out my tax situation; sort out my filing; sort out my address system; get fit; eat better; spend more time with my family.

We decided to work on the filing, tax and address book issues, as these were directly work related. I spoke to the coach once a week for three months. Each time at the end of the conversation he set me a task (e.g. throw away or move two of the lamps and buy a stock of bulbs for the one that worked). Amazingly I found that after I had completed each task some of the weight lifted off my shoulders and I felt energized to start another task.

Now, three months later, my office is still a bit of a mess but much better than it was. I have joined a gym, lost 7lbs, take on fewer assignments that I didn't really want to do, have paid my tax bill, and even feel I have more time to spend with my family. I have learnt to say no to things I don't really want to do.

It all sounds straightforward and is probably only common sense, but having someone on the other end of the phone to work out these problems with has allowed me to move forward and change the things I don't want to put up with.

The most amazing thing is that I have found time to go back to my music. I hadn't opened the piano for about two years but I happened to meet a teacher who was prepared to take on adults and now I'm having lessons once a week. It seems incredible that I have left it all this time when it is a source of such pleasure to me.

It sounds odd but almost for the first time in my life I am starting to feel in control.'

Mark, 43, concert promoter

Can you coach yourself?

If you work through the programme presented at the back of this book, you will make changes in your life. If you follow the programme, it will work. It may be hard to keep yourself on track and if this is the case you may decide to co-coach (*see* Chapter 10). The techniques do work, but change is not easy and you will need courage and determination to succeed.

Above all, coaching is about learning and change. It is about increasing your motivation, telling your own story, creating your own dreams. Coaching is more about asking questions than giving answers. By becoming your own life coach you will learn to:

◆ clarify your purpose and values

◆ reinvent or rediscover yourself

◆ develop and carry out action plans

◆ ask the right questions – the answers will come.

Coaching is about change and transformation. It:

◆ opens up possibilities

◆ works on behavioural and emotional levels

◆ focuses on results.

'I turned to coaching because I felt unfulfilled in my life. I had tried all sorts of ideas and therapies before, including counselling, drama therapy and yoga. Each one had worked to some extent but I still felt my life was in a bit of a mess. Perhaps it was because I am getting older, but I increasingly had the feeling that there should be more to life than this.

I didn't want to work with a coach, partly because I couldn't afford it but also because I just didn't want to spend time telling someone else about all the things that were wrong with my life. Perhaps I am just arrogant but I felt I could fix things myself.

I have to say I found it very straightforward. I started to use the life-coaching techniques I had read about and things started to fall into place.

The most powerful part was the bit about focusing on success. In a way that is what you do when you write up your CV. You write down all the things you've done in your life and suddenly you think, "Well yes – I have achieved a lot, haven't I."

And I found it worked even with little things. For example, I went to a dance class at my gym and although I was terrible at it I really loved it. Some of the other people in the class had been professional dancers and I was just bumbling about at the back.

I was on the point of giving up but I decided to do a sort of "success" profile on myself. I knew that I had a good sense of rhythm, I had learned that at school. And because I had done yoga I was pretty flexible. So I thought, well that's a pretty good start, why don't I give it a bit longer. I promised myself to go to ten classes before I gave up. By the end of the ten classes I was improving and I decided to keep going.

And I sort of went through each area of my life, applying the techniques and making changes.

The most helpful thing was understanding the process of change. Before I found out about these techniques I thought that not being able to change the things I didn't like meant that I was just weak willed. But once I understood that change is quite a complicated process, I was less hard on myself. I sort of see myself on a continuous journey towards success. I might never actually get there, but then what would getting there mean anyway?

I just know that I feel more in control of my life now and I have started to believe that I can steer things in the direction I want to go.'

Delores, 36, housing executive

STEP ONE

An irritations inventory

Task: do an irritations inventory on your life. Identify areas of discomfort, aspects of your life that you are tolerating but that are causing you problems.

STEP TWO

Select an area to work on

Task: choose two or three of these areas to work on.

coach yourself

chapter two

03

chapter three
all change
what works and what doesn't

Change is difficult

Whenever we change from one type of behaviour or situation to another, we are losing something as well as gaining.[1] It is this loss that can be difficult to cope with, no matter how unhelpful or unproductive the behaviour we are leaving behind.

But some people do manage to make successful changes in their lives, under the most difficult circumstances, with and without professional help. People can and do change careers, give up abusive behaviour, overcome tremendous obstacles to achieve their goals, leaving the rest of us filled with awe and admiration asking, 'How do they do it?'

In recent years psychologists have done a lot of research into how people create change. We all know it isn't easy, but if we can understand how successful changers do it, perhaps we can borrow some of their techniques to bring about the changes we want to make in our own lives.

Michael was an oil trader who had always dreamed of writing and travelling but had never had the courage to leave his comfortable life. He had made several attempts at starting a novel and was attending an evening class on creative writing. Suddenly, tragically, his wife died and he was left wondering what life was all about. He found he could hardly cope with his terrible loss. He was so distressed that he took some months off work and threw himself into his writing. He finished the novel, found an agent, sold the book plus the film rights for a massive sum, and is now a full-time author.

For Michael it was a terrible and tragic event that pushed him to make the change in his life. We can hope not to be driven by such loss. But it was not the loss of his wife that made Michael want to be a writer. That was a dream he had had for a long time. It was the awful events in his life that made him take the leap. Luck, talent and determination helped him to succeed, but the desire to write was already there.

Contemplating change

Most people who make changes spend a considerable amount of time thinking about change before they actually do anything. This is encouraging. The fact that you've been dreaming about a change for a long time, even making some attempts at change but not succeeding is not a reason to feel despondent or to give up. Rather it seems that this 'contemplation phase' is part of the change process.

Thoughts, feelings, behaviour and situations

In order to sustain real and lasting change in our lives we need to change thoughts, feelings and behaviour. We also need to set up the situation or our environment so that we are supported in making change. Changing just one of these four will not bring us the results we want or at least the change will not last for very long. If we only change our behaviour but continue to think negatively about what we are doing, it will not be very long before we start to feel as if we can't continue and we will probably give up. If we only change our thoughts and feelings, there's no guarantee our behaviour will change. We also need to take time to structure the situation or environment to support us in making change.

It's a bit like building a house (see Figure 3.1). If we don't pay attention to building all four corners of the structure, the roof won't be supported and the house may collapse.

We will look at techniques for doing this in Chapter 6.

GOAL

Situation ← → Behaviour

Thoughts ← → Emotions

Figure 3.1 The house of change – a structure to support change in our lives

Understanding change

Many people think that making changes is simply a matter of making a decision, but if it were that easy why are hospitals full of people whose unhealthy lifestyle has made them ill, or is even killing them? Why would we continue to act in ways that make us feel bad about ourselves? Why would dieting and weight loss be a multi-million-dollar industry? The fact is, making purposeful, directed change is complicated.

Sam works as a picture researcher for a web-site design company. He likes his job but feels bad about his lifestyle. He knows he should get more exercise, give up smoking and eat more healthily. Every few months or so he gets depressed about his physical condition and starts an exercise regime.

When he sets out on one of these regimes he is usually very determined and wants quick results. He resolves to get up early every day and spend an hour at the gym before work, to go on a strict low-fat diet and to give up beer. Sometimes he manages this regime for a few weeks and he does sometimes lose weight. But he finds the regime tough. He finds it very difficult to get up at six (the time he has set himself) and he gets bad-tempered and irritable because he restricts his diet so much that he is always hungry. Sooner or later he slips, gives up the exercise and goes back to his old habits.

Every time he fails in this way he feels worse about himself. His negative self-talk says:

'I'm just a slob'

'I'll never lose weight'

'I'm fat and ugly'.

He ends up feeling worse about himself than before he started. Eventually he doesn't even want to try to get fit any more because he knows he will end up feeling terrible.

Sometimes the changes we need to make are just small ones – leave the house five minutes earlier, make the bed before you leave in the morning, listen more carefully when other people are talking, eat more vegetables, exercise more regularly. Sometimes they are momentous, life-time decisions – change career, move house, leave your partner, have a baby. Whatever the circumstance, all change is accompanied by ambivalence, and ambivalence can be very uncomfortable. Making any kind of decision can be difficult if you cannot cope with feelings of regret. When you choose one thing you automatically lose something else, and you have to be able to cope with that loss. But it is exhausting and impossible to keep all your options open all the time. You have to make decisions. Choose one thing and move on. You can always choose something else the next time. If you spend your time continually toying with the alternatives, you will never be able to move forward.

Like most other things decision making gets better with practice.

Like most other things decision-making gets better with practice. Exercise your decision-making muscle and it will get stronger. The problem with making decisions is that decisions change the path of our lives and no one can tell us which is the best path to follow. We have to find that out for ourselves.

'As soon as questions of will or decision or reason or choice of action arise, human science is at a loss.'

Noam Chomsky, American linguist and political activist, TV interview, 30 March 1978

It's never too late

If you understand the process of change you will begin to see that change is possible at any age, no matter what your background and experience. People can and do manage to make enormous and inspirational changes in their lives.

It is so easy to feel that we are too old, too set in our ways to change, but this is not true. Many people make changes and achieve remarkable things later in life. The Russian writer Leo Tolstoy learned to ride a bicycle at the age of 67, much to the shock and annoyance of his friends and family.

'Tolstoy has learned to ride a bicycle. Is this not inconsistent with his Christian ideals?'

Friend

Tolstoy himself saw nothing wrong in his new hobby.

'I don't know why I like it. N. is offended and finds fault with me for doing this but I keep on doing it and am not ashamed. On the contrary, I feel that I am entitled to my share of natural light-heartedness, that the opinion of others is of no importance, and that there is nothing wrong in enjoying oneself simply, like a boy.'

Leo Tolstoy

Not bad when you're nearly 70 (and that's not to mention the novels).

Jeanne Calment, who lived to be 122 and was still riding a bicycle at the age of 100 (we don't know when she learned), gave up smoking at the age of 117. Interviewed on her 120th birthday in 1995 she said: 'I've waited 110 years to be famous, I plan to enjoy it for as long as possible.'

Of course, neither Tolstoy nor Jeanne Calment knew about life coaching but they both managed to make changes in their lives at an advanced age. And if you look you can find countless examples of people who have made changes or achieved great things later in life.

People give all sorts of reasons why they can't make changes. They blame it on their childhood, their genes, their age, their circumstances. In fact, the reason we can't make changes is often because we simply don't understand the mechanisms.

Model of change

Since 1984 there have been more than 500 articles on the 'stages of change' published in the academic press, which show that change is a complex, dynamic process with six or seven stages. Psychologists James O. Prochaska, John C. Norcross and Carlo C. DiClemente[2] have been writing about and studying how people change for more than 20 years. They have developed a model of the change process. It is quite simple to understand and can be applied to almost any area of our lives.

The model can be represented as a diagram (Figure 3.2) in which our actions are seen as part of a continuous loop.

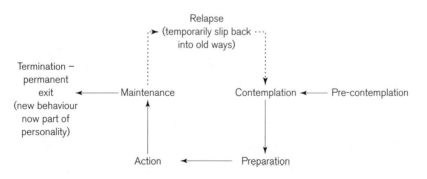

Figure 3.2 A model of change

- *Pre-contemplation* is the stage before we even start to think about making change.

- We enter the model from the right-hand side when we start to think about change. This is the *contemplation* stage. The main feeling we will experience here is ambivalence. We want things to change but at the same time we want them to stay the same.

- If despite our reservations we continue to think about change, we will probably enter the *preparation* stage. At this point we have made the decision to change whatever it is we are fed up with although we still feel quite unsure whether it is really what we want.

- After preparation comes *action* when we actually start to take some steps towards change.

- Then we enter the *maintenance* stage.

- If we are successful in changing our behaviour we *exit* the model on the left-hand side and the new behaviours have become a part of our personality and our daily life.

- *Relapse* is where we end up (once again) doing the very thing we've been trying so hard to change. The key point is that relapse is a normal part of change.

We will probably feel some ambivalence throughout the process. There will always be some reasons for staying where we are. Leaving the comfort zone is always difficult, even if the change is for the better.

Relapse is normal

However determined we are to change, what often happens is that at some point in the cycle we relapse and slip back into old forms of behaviour. Relapse is a very normal part of the change process. It becomes damaging to progress only if it lowers our self-esteem so much that we end up giving up on the change completely.

If we can acknowledge and accept that relapse is a normal and expected – perhaps even necessary – part of the change process, we can use it to strengthen our determination.

Different approaches

There are many different ways of bringing about change. A therapist or counsellor may be the answer for some people; family and friends very often provide important help and support. But it is not only those who have professional help who manage to change, and not everyone who has professional help does manage to make the changes they want to make. People find their own ways of making changes, some more successful than others. A therapist or counsellor will usually try to help you to understand the problem behaviour and for some people this may be important. But understanding is not changing and sometimes we can change without fully understanding why we are behaving as we are. We will look at this more fully in Chapter 7.

Costs and benefits

Research shows that throughout the cycle of change we weigh up the costs and benefits of change. When the benefits seem to outweigh the costs we take action.

What does the research show?

A group of psychologists in the United States carried out a research programme on 12 problem behaviours including smoking, lack of exercise, eating a high-fat diet, and illegal drug use. Their studies showed that the pattern of change was the same across all 12 behaviours and that subjects did seem to go through the stages of change we describe above. The pattern of weighing up costs and benefits was consistent across the group, with the benefits increasing and the costs decreasing as subjects moved from pre-contemplation to contemplation, decision, action, and maintenance.[3]

At each stage of the cycle we will find ourselves weighing up the costs and benefits of change. For example, before he starts his exercise programme Sam is in two minds. He wants to get fit but he doesn't want to give up his easygoing lifestyle. There are benefits to staying as he is and doing nothing. It is easier for a start. But the fact that he has decided to make a change means that in his mind the benefits of an exercise programme outweigh the costs.

He has already decided to take action and has achieved a degree of success. But because the regime he imposes on himself is so harsh, the costs of the programme seem to be outweighing the benefits and he gives up.

He needs to carefully plan himself a programme where the benefits increase all the time and the costs decrease. The costs may never vanish altogether; he may always have to put a bit of effort into keeping fit. But he is much more likely to be successful if he doesn't ask too much of himself.

Monitoring

How will Sam know what 'asking too much' is? Well, the only way of doing this is to continually monitor your progress.[4] Sam must build some mechanism into his fitness regime that allows him to see how well he's doing, how easy or difficult he's finding it, and to adjust his plan accordingly.

Sam could stay in the trying and failing to get fit loop for a long time. If he is to move out of the loop he needs to change his behaviour, thoughts and feelings and adjust his environment or situation to support his change. It is perfectly possible, but he may need help to find the strategies that will work for him.

What he needs to do is:

◆ look at the areas where he is successful

◆ focus on his achievements

◆ picture the way he would like his life to be

◆ set himself some realistic, achievable goals

◆ allow himself to fail sometimes without turning it into a catastrophe

◆ enlist the support of friends

◆ take small steps towards his goals

- structure his life to help him attain his goals
- chart his progress
- reward himself for his successes.

Acknowledging success

In fact, Sam is successful in lots of areas of his life.

- He is very good at his job and has won industry prizes for some of his designs.
- He is very popular and has lots of friends.
- He is a good communicator and team player and is good at motivating others to get the job done.
- He works very hard at his job. When there is extra work to do it is often Sam who is prepared to put in the extra time, to go the extra mile. He isn't lazy at all at work.
- In the past he has managed to lose weight and get fit.
- It is true he is slightly overweight but it is his poor self-image and consequent lack of pride in his appearance that makes him look a bit shabby and slobbish. He likes clothes and has a good eye for design and colour. He could look much better than he does.

Achieving balance

Sam would like to have more balance in his life. Because he is good at what he does and because he is by nature a compassionate person, he spends a lot of time helping other people with difficult work tasks. He finds it hard to say no to some of his colleagues' demands. This sometimes makes him feel resentful. He dreams of a life where he has more time for himself and his own interests and where sometimes people are helping and supporting him instead of the other way round.

Realistic goals

Sam needs to think about what his goals for fitness are and to try to set himself some goals that fit in with his values and self-image.

Failure – or useful feedback

Because Sam is hard on himself he feels bad if he fails to live up to his own rather high standards. If he could allow himself some leeway, and to fail occasionally, he might feel more successful overall. In fact, if Sam reconsiders the whole idea of failure as being feedback which allows him to fine-tune his action plans, then failure becomes just another source of information which helps him to reach his goals.

Enlisting support

Sam is liked and admired by lots of people. There is probably more help and support available for him than he realizes. He needs to allow himself to make some demands on his colleagues and friends. He has certainly earned it. Also, if he allowed people to give something back, he would feel less resentful for all the help he gives them.

Start small

There are probably some tiny steps that Sam can take towards changing his lifestyle. He could start walking to work, wait until 10.30 to have his first cigarette, make sure that the computer manuals are easily available for people who have been bothering him with simple problems. He could also put up some visual signs as cues to remind him of the benefits of quitting.

Charting progress

He definitely needs to develop some sort of system of charting his progress towards his goals. He could use a daily, weekly or monthly journal to plan his fitness and exercise programme. Research shows that diary keeping helps us to make sense of unorganized information and helps us reach our goals more quickly and easily.

What does the research show?

Research carried out at the University of South Carolina[5] showed that the way managers recorded information about their subordinates' performance at work affected the way they appraised the performance.

If they organized the information according to the person, their appraisals were more accurate than if they organized their information according to the tasks they completed.

The implications of this are that if we organize and record information in a particular way it could help us to be more accurate and specific in reaching our goals.

Rewards

As he reaches his goals Sam needs to reward himself.[6] In this way he acknowledges what he has achieved and it becomes less likely that he will fall back into the kind of negative self-talk that he is prone to.[7]

Weighing up the costs

One way to decide whether or not any particular change of behaviour is what you really want is to carry out a decisional balance; in other words, weigh up the costs of change against the benefits. This is the sort of thing you do in your head every day when trying to choose between two options.

'If I stay in I'll get an early night and feel refreshed in the morning.'
'If I go out I might meet some interesting people and have a great time.'

But you can make this activity explicit and actually write down the costs and benefits of any action.

Negative effects in my life that will be caused by failure to achieve my goals	Positive effects in my life when I do achieve my goals
I'll feel bad about myself.	I will feel better, have more energy.
I might find it harder to find a partner.	I will be healthier.
My health will suffer.	I might have more girlfriends.

In Sam's case it is pretty straightforward. The positive side looks much better.

This example is simple but you can use this technique for all sorts of areas of your life.

Max works for an events organizer company. He loves his job because it is stimulating and varied and he gets to meet a lot of people. He works with a great team and they all work very hard. He is doing well at his job and is offered promotion. His boss wants him to be co-ordinator for his team. Max is pleased but quite cautious. He is one of the youngest members of the company and he is worried about how the others will feel about him being in charge. He has never been in charge of other people before and he is worried that he will lose the closeness and the fun of his job at the moment.

Even changes for the better can be daunting.

Even changes for the better can be daunting and can cause a great deal of stress. This is not a change that Max has chosen himself, and he finds the prospect of being in charge daunting. He will be paid more money of course, but otherwise he is much more aware of the costs of the new position (losing the camaraderie of working with the team) than the benefits.

He probably needs to sit down with his boss and discuss his fears and work out strategies for coping with the new position. It might be helpful for him to list the benefits of the new job and decide if it really is what he wants.

So what does work?

Research confirms what most of us might know instinctively. If you plan your change carefully you are more likely to be successful.

What does the research show?

You are more likely to be successful in making changes in your life if you spend some time thinking about your aims. By weighing up the advantages and disadvantages, and planning how you will carry out the changes, you are already moving yourself closer to making changes. Clinical tests showed that people who carried out these 'pre-change' activities were more successful in making changes in their lives than people who didn't.

To move yourself closer to change you need to:

◆ weigh up the advantages and disadvantages

◆ plan your strategy

◆ decide when, where and how you are going to achieve your aims.

From weighing to willing: approaching a change decision through pre- or post-decisional motivation[8]

Some people make very big changes in their lives but the sort of emotions and uncertainties they go through are probably the same.

Remy and Monica have lived abroad for several years. They set off from their native Australia in their mid-20s, wanting to travel a bit before settling down. After travelling in Europe, they came to London, liked it and decided to stay for a bit. They both found jobs and after some time it seemed to make financial sense to buy a house instead of renting.

They had their first child, a little girl, in London, followed two years later by a boy. The children grew older and their daughter Natalie started school. The question of whether and when to return to Australia was always on their minds but at the same time they were happy and settled in their adopted country.

Eventually their homesickness and longing for a more outdoor life grew so great that they decided to return to Australia. This is what their decisional balance looked like just before they left England.

Benefits of staying

◆ The children are happy.

◆ We love our house.

◆ We have lots of friends.

◆ It is stimulating and exciting to live in a big European city.

◆ Monica is a writer; there might be more opportunities in London.

Benefits of going

◆ More time with family and old friends.

◆ Children get to see more of their grandparents.

◆ Live a freer, more outdoor life.

◆ Could live in a beautiful part of the city.

◆ More relaxed lifestyle.

- Ease the aching homesickness we sometimes feel.

- The children might have a better future, more opportunities.

- Our families, in particular the grandparents, will be pleased.

- Monica's parents suffer from ill health and need some help.

It is not an easy decision for them but in the end they go back to Sydney, where they came from, but decide to move to a new suburb, one where neither of them knows anyone.

After some months they find that although happy to be home, they are still not quite satisfied. In this kind of change, relapse is rather difficult because the move has been made and to go back to London would be very difficult. But the way they might and indeed do experience relapse is through regret and uncertainty. It is almost inevitable that at times they will doubt their decision to leave England. If they allow themselves to feel regret and understand that it is a normal part of the change process, they are much more likely to be able to settle happily into their new lives.

Bereavement, injury, separation, redundancy, new relationships, jobs or relocation radically change our lives. Good events as well as bad shake us up and require us to alter our view of the world. It takes time and effort to readjust. If we understand and deal with the crises that are caused by changes in our lives, we can turn traumatic events into turning points and opportunities.

Money matters

Money is an emotive issue for the vast majority of people. It is almost impossible to have a neutral attitude to money. Money is one of the most common causes of fights within marriages and between partners. Given that it is such an emotional issue, financial habits and assumptions are of course some of the hardest to change.

Pete is hopeless with money. He earns a lot in his job as accounts manager for a large advertising agency, but he always spends a bit more than he's got. He loves cars and feels he needs to drive something quite impressive. He has a large mortgage on his flat and always takes expensive holidays. He wears good clothes and likes to eat out. He also mixes with a crowd of rather well-heeled friends. He is slipping further and further into debt and he is beginning to realize he will have to do something about it.

He decides to make an appointment with a financial advisor who may be able to help him. He thinks that perhaps by increasing his mortgage or juggling his credit card bills he may be able to ease things a bit. The financial advisor immediately sees that he is in a very bad situation and in fact could be in danger of losing his home.

Pete is advised to cut up his credit cards, sell his car and buy a cheaper one, make a plan for paying off his debts, monitor his expenditure and generally tighten his belt.

He is doing well for a few weeks (although he doesn't sell the car). Then he meets a new girlfriend. He is so desperate to impress her that some of his old habits start creeping up on him. Before long he is slipping back into the cycle of debt and overspending. This time he starts opening a lot of store cards to buy new clothes and spending a lot of money on clubs and restaurants.

Pete is locked into a very deeply entrenched cycle of behaviour, thoughts and feelings. If he is going to make a change and deal with his finances in a way that he feels better about, he is going to have to work very hard at making some changes. Coaching techniques could help him to set himself some clear goals and to achieve them. As he is also a gregarious and sociable man, he may find that co-coaching – making a commitment to work with someone else – will help him (*see* Chapter 10).

By monitoring his progress, accepting relapse, and finding someone to help, he has a good chance of making some lasting change.

Ambivalence is normal

The most enduring state we find ourselves in at the beginning of the change process is ambivalence. We want to change and we don't. We want to get fit, and we want to just slob out. We want to end the relationship, and we want to stay where we are. We want to start that new course, but we don't want the hassle of all the work. This is completely normal, in fact almost inevitable. We don't know what the new behaviour will mean.

'Fear ... is forward. No one is afraid of yesterday.' Renata Adler[97]

As we move through the stages of change we should find that our feeling of ambivalence decreases. The pluses start to outweigh the minuses. But it is important to remember that feelings of ambivalence may never go away altogether. When we make a change there might always be moments, however brief, when we wish we had stayed as we were. This is a normal part of being alive. There is always some part of us that is going to wonder what might have been. By acknowledging this we can accept and welcome change into our lives.

Ian was a smoker for 40 years. At the age of 62 he suffered a serious heart attack. His doctor warned him that he must stop smoking, which he did, successfully. A friend he hadn't seen for a couple of years came to visit and asked him how he was managing.

Ian said to him, somewhat wryly: 'Well, I have to admit that the quality of my life has definitely gone down.'

Ian was probably healthier and fitter than he had been for years. In real terms the quality of his life had improved enormously. The fact was that he was *alive* which might not have been the case if he had continued smoking. But by jokingly acknowledging his loss and accepting it as part of his life, he is much more likely to be able to sustain his position as a non-smoker than if he tried to pretend to himself and the world that he didn't miss it at all.

Small steps

One big reason why many people fail to make changes in their lives is that they try to do too much too quickly. We look at setting SMART goals in the next chapter, but for now try to make some tiny changes in your life. Try to make just one small change in each of the following areas:

◆ your work space

◆ your car

◆ your kitchen

◆ your wardrobe

◆ this week's reading material

◆ your eating habits.

If there is something that you know you need to do but have been putting off (tidying your work space, redecorating a room, writing a letter), try spending just 10 minutes a day on it for one week. See how far you get. You may even be motivated to carry on.

'True life is lived when tiny changes occur.'   Leo Tolstoy

STEP THREE

Understand change

Work out where you are in the change cycle.

Pre-contemplation – I haven't been thinking about making changes in this area and I don't intend to in the near future.

Contemplation – I have thought about making changes in this area of my life, but haven't actually done anything about it yet.

Preparation – I am going to make a change but I'm not quite sure if it's the right thing to do.

Action – I have been actively making real changes in this area of my life for at least the last month.

Maintenance – I have been actively making successful changes in this area for about six months.

Relapse – I had started to make real changes but I seem to have slipped back into my old ways.

chapter four
hopes and dreams
what do you really want?

'Go confidently in the direction of your dreams. Live the life you've imagined.'
Henry David Thoreau (1817–1862), US essayist, poet, naturalist

You've got to have a dream

To create change in your life the first thing you have to do is dream. Dream of your future. Dream of what you want. Imagine your life as you feel it ought to be lived. This is as true for small changes in your life as for bigger ones. Research has shown that people who want to lose weight are much more successful if they can picture themselves looking as they want to look.[1] People who try to stop smoking are told to *see* themselves as 'non-smokers'.[2] Not knowing what the future holds is very stressful. One of the most difficult and stressful times for patients is the time between undergoing tests and getting the results. Once we know the results we can start to adjust, however bad the news, but while we are waiting we don't know what sort of future we are facing.

We need to be able to imagine a future for ourselves. This is part of what gives us the will to live. Luis Buñuel, one of the most celebrated and controversial film-makers of the 20th century, says in his autobiography: 'Life without memory is no life at all, just as an intelligence without the possibility of expression is not really an intelligence. Our memory is our coherence, or reason, our feeling, even our action. Without it we are nothing.'[3]

But equally, being able to imagine and plan the future is part of what makes us human. We cannot escape the past, and we cannot avoid the future; instead we must make both future and past work for us. We must learn to tell the story of our lives the way we want it to be told and this means living life the way we want to live it.

Fuzzy vision

We may not necessarily fulfil our dreams precisely, but we need a general sense of the sort of life we want to be leading and the direction we want to be travelling in. Our dreams cannot be too rigid and immovable because life changes, the unexpected happens and has to be incorporated into our lives.

In 1953 Sir Edmund Hillary led the team that conquered Mount Everest. In interviews he made it clear that climbing the highest mountain in the world had not been a life-long ambition or dream, but that he had always known that he wanted, and needed, an adventurous life.

'My dreams were almost all adventurous dreams. I was not lonely, but I didn't really have many friends, and I used to go on long walks. I was a very keen walker and, as I walked along the roads and tracks around this countryside area, I'd be dreaming. My mind would be miles away and I would be slashing villains with swords and capturing beautiful maidens and doing all sorts of heroic things, just purely in my dreams. I used to love to walk for hours and hours and my mind would be far away in all sorts of heroic efforts.'

Sir Edmund Hillary, talking about his childhood in San Francisco, 16 November 1991

You've got to know where you're going or you'll never know if you've got there. On the other hand, too clear a picture of what you want to achieve can be demotivating. You can use up all your energy focusing on a rigid picture of the future and in doing so you may well miss the opportunities and chances that life offers you. Great achievers usually have a vision that they will succeed, but perhaps not too clear a vision. In fact, to succeed perhaps we need to develop *fuzzy vision.*

'I was never one of those people who, at an early age, had picked an objective and worked steadily towards it. All I knew was that I wanted to get involved in adventurous activity. I didn't have any specific type of activity in mind, but I wanted to do things that were exciting and adventurous. I had a fairly diffused feeling as to what precisely it should be … I never had a vision to climb Mount Everest. As with everything else it just more or less grew … Never in my early days did I ever think of attempting to reach the summit of Mount Everest.' Sir Edmund Hillary

But perhaps to be worthwhile dreams must be something that are slightly out of reach, something worth striving for.

'Si l'on sait exactement ce que l'on va faire, a quoi bon le faire?' (If you know EXACTLY what you are going to do, what is the point of doing it?) Pablo Picasso

It is not always easy to know what we do want, what our dreams really are. But there are techniques you can use to help you to get hold of what it is you want from life.

Imagining the future

Formula one racing drivers use two kinds of information when they drive in Grand Prix races: feedback and feedforward. Feedback tells them exactly what is happening at that precise moment. If a car swerves in front of them or if someone is overtaking them, it is feedback information that allows them to respond. But they drive their cars at such high speeds that it would be impossible to rely on feedback information to steer their way round the track. By the time a driver's brain has told him that there is a curve in the road, it is too late to react. He has to know beforehand. This is where feedforward comes in. Racing drivers study the tracks before they race and they practise many times on the track before taking part in a competition. So they know the outline of the track very well before they race. Their brains use this information to steer a course round the track. They are looking to the exit of the curve as they enter it, focusing ahead all the time with the automatic part of their minds. This leaves the conscious decision-making part of their minds to deal with immediate adjustments and crises.

So in a very real sense racing drivers can race well only by imagining and picturing what is coming next. They have a clear view of where they want to go, but they also have to have finely tuned reactions to deal with situations as they occur.

Everyday learner drivers do not have the automatic reactions and 'feel' for the car that more experienced drivers have. They cannot look at the road ahead to deal with what is coming up. They use all their effort to steer a course between the kerb and the middle of the road. It is only with practice that they learn to trust their judgement about how to drive the car and deal with events on the road as they occur.

Musicians do the same thing. They play one part of the piece while looking forward on the score, reading the bit coming up.

If you live your life without any view of where you want to go you will spend all your time and energy just steering yourself slowly round the course. If you take some time to imagine and plan some kind of future for yourself, you free up your conscious mind to deal with and enjoy the day-to-day decisions and experiences.

Of course, none of us can actually predict the future.

Of course, none of us can actually predict the future, we can't know what is going to happen to us, but we can formulate a picture of the sort of future we would like. We can at least decide what is important to us and what we want to focus on. One method of doing this is to write yourself a letter from the future.

Letter from the future

At first this might seem like a strange, even uncomfortable exercise. In fact, although simple to do, it is a powerful tool. Many people, including the senior leadership team of the Royal Australian Air Force test pilots, captains of industry, school teachers, builders, construction workers and accountants, have used it successfully. It is all very well to say you have to dream, but many of us don't even know what our dreams are, can't say exactly what we want from life. By writing a letter from your future self you can help yourself to tap into the issues and achievements that are important to you.[4] It can help you to work out what your values are and where you want to be.

What does the research show?

Research shows that individuals who are feeling anxious are more likely to notice whatever it is they perceive to be a threat than those who are feeling relaxed.[5] So if you are afraid of spiders you are more likely to notice them than if you aren't afraid. Your anxiety 'primes' you to notice the threat.

The letter from the future helps you to create a bright future for yourself by priming you to notice opportunities. Once you set these expectations for yourself you are more likely to achieve them.

Procedure

Choose a date some months or even years ahead, a date that means something to you – an anniversary or a birthday. Then imagine that your life has gone rather well. Things have turned out the way you wanted them to. Write yourself a letter telling your about the developments in your life. Try to imagine how your life would feel if you were successful and fulfilled. The best way to understand how to do this exercise is to look at a few examples of other people who have done it.

Gary is a senior fire officer in a large city. He lives with his partner and two small children. This is what he says about his life before he wrote himself the letter:

'For most of my adult life I have been conscious of the need to be seen as successful. I suppose, like most people I know, I measure most of my success and happiness by material wealth. My career has been the means to achieve my material goals; promotion equals more money. Once I have achieved one target or set of targets, I immediately set new ones that are generally more difficult and involve more commitment. This leads to longer hours in the office, more residential courses, and has been responsible for an overall imbalance between my career and domestic life.

▶

This lifestyle sometimes leaves me wondering where it will all end. I always seem to be on a journey to another goal, always living in the future. But now I am reaching my mid-30s I am beginning to wonder what it is that I really want. I have already attained a senior management position and I don't feel so hungry to chase further promotion every time the opportunity arises. I am in a long-term relationship and I have two young children. In practical terms this means that I leave the house before the children are awake and often don't arrive back home until after they are in bed. Even on the days that I do arrive home early it is always a struggle to engage the children fully as I feel so physically and emotionally tired.

For the first time in my life I am beginning to consider whether I've got my priorities right. I am beginning to wonder what it is that is so important to me and those around me. Why do I work such long hours? Why do I allow my work to be all-consuming when there is so much more to living?

These feelings and the desire to address the imbalance in my life are proving to be the catalyst for change and are leading me to challenge my own values.'

You may think that someone involved in such a traditionally 'tough', male occupation would find this 'letter from the future' business a bit soft. But Gary was prepared for it. In recent years the fire service has begun to acknowledge and recognize that we all, especially those doing stressful, sometimes traumatic jobs such as the emergency services, need to learn ways to deal with our emotions. We need ways of coping with our busy, stressful lives.

As fire fighters move up the organization they move away from the team. They can no longer sit with their work mates after each emergency, and talk and joke their way towards dealing with what they have done and seen. The informal mechanisms are not there for the senior managers, they have to find some way of coping with their feelings in a more structured way. At the same time, as with any modern organization, the pressures on them are immense.

For some time the fire service has been providing courses for senior fire officers designed to help them to cope with the stress of their jobs. On these courses they are taught the benefits of relaxation, meditation and the importance of emotional intelligence at work.

The fire service is only one example and in some ways an extreme one. Fire fighters are dealing with things that the rest of us can hope never to have to experience. But as the pace of life speeds up we all have to learn to cope with stress. We have to learn to tap into and cope with the feelings that are produced by our frenetic lives.

Traditional management training which concentrates on acquisition of specific, measurable skills hasn't alleviated the stresses of modern living and working. In order for organizations to remain flexible, modern and efficient, they have to create mechanisms for the workforce to understand, acknowledge and deal constructively with their emotions.[6] The costs to the individual of not acknowledging these feelings are illness, depression and even breakdown.[7] The cost to the fire service is lost working days or losing staff who have been expensively recruited and trained.

Within the fire service there is another layer of complexity. If they are to be proactive – preventing accidents and fires before they start – rather than reactive, they need to work with the community. In most large cities the community comprises a huge ethnic and cultural mix. In order to work with the community, the fire service must represent and reflect it. This means that the organization must be welcoming to women and ethnic minorities. This involves an acceptance of individual strengths and weaknesses and different emotional styles. In order to do this you have to get in touch with your emotions and find your own ways of coping with crises. It all sounds soft and vague, but the reality is hard and pragmatic. If the service understands and reflects the community, they can work with it. If they can work with the community, they can prevent fires. If they prevent fires, they save lives.

Here is the letter Gary wrote himself.

'Now, two years on, I am pleased to say that I feel more content with my life. I have finally broken the "doing" and "having" cycle and I now live in the present. I am more

▶

disciplined with my work commitments, ensuring that I have quality time to share with my family and friends.

Although work is still important to me it is no longer the dominant factor in my life. I now recognize the importance of doing what I want rather than living up to the expectations of others. I am comfortable with this new approach and actively encourage and support my work colleagues to review their life in the same way. I also feel confident to openly discuss my needs and desires with my employers. This honesty has given my line managers a better understanding of me as a person and has afforded me a different kind of respect.

This new approach has also required me to review my working priorities. I no longer believe that promotion should be attained at the expense of everything else. By accepting this I have removed the pressure that I always used to put on myself. I no longer feel that I am on a never-ending quest for self-actualization. In fact, if anything, I have become more reflective and take satisfaction from what I have already achieved. This is not to say that I have become complacent. Instead I focus on aspects of my work that I can influence and/or control. This has removed a significant amount of stress from my life and given me more time to concentrate on work that falls within my sphere of influence. I also haven't lost my appetite for further development/promotion. I am just waiting until the time is right for both me and my family to make the commitment.

I now place less value on material gain and have taken a more holistic appreciation of life. This ensures that my professional commitments complement and support rather than conflict and undermine the rest of my life. To this end I now work more locally, which has given me greater flexibility with my time and has cut out many of the stresses associated with commuting into the centre of town.

The newly created spare time is primarily spent at home with my family. This has afforded me quality time with my children and has allowed me to support my partner with the routine challenges of family life. To some this may not seem particularly profound or significant, but to me and my family this shared time is invaluable. It has allowed me to develop my relationship with my children and has given me opportunities to watch them mature and actively assist in their development. The extra time spent with my partner is also more relaxed as she no longer feels that she is coping with the children on her own. The mere fact that I am home at a reasonable time somehow appears to diminish the daily tensions of family life. It has also allowed me to support my partner's life balance as she now has more time and flexibility to pursue her own needs and interests.

As I have already mentioned, I now recognize that material wealth is no guarantee of happiness. While deep down I have always known this fact, it is only recently that I have come to appreciate how I can apply this belief to my own life. I now take more interest in my spiritual well-being and regularly meditate. I not only find this mentally and physically relaxing, it also makes me more aware of my feelings. I am now more in touch with my emotions and find it easier to express them.

Having developed the ability to understand my own needs and aspirations I have also become more aware and sensitive to the needs of others. To this end I am more easy-going and less judgemental. I now look for and value the positive qualities of others and readily accept people for who they are. In general, I have become more intrigued by people and the different approaches to life. I am fascinated to find out how others balance their existence and to what extent they are true to their own values and beliefs.

If I was asked to sum up what has changed in my life I would say that I have taken control and regained the balance.'

Of course, just having a vision or a dream of a future life is not enough to get us there. In order to do that we need to set targets, and chart our progress towards them. If Gary is to reach the balanced life he dreams of he is going to have to work pretty hard and set himself some very clear goals. We will look at specific techniques for doing this in Chapter 5. But first we must have a dream of what we want, a hope for the future. Writing yourself a letter allows you to look at all aspects of your life and identify the things that are important to you.

Writing yourself a letter allows you to look at all aspects of your life.

Remy and Monica have recently returned to live in their native city of Sydney, Australia, after eight years in England. The decision to leave England was a difficult one, but eventually the pull of home was too strong for them. Now, eight months on, they are quite settled but not without regrets.

Monica in particular found it hard to leave all her friends and her rich and full life in London. The place they now live in is a very beautiful suburb on the coast north of Sydney, but it is more isolated than the bustling part of London they moved from.

Monica is at quite a low point when she decides to write the letter, feeling hemmed in and unfulfilled. The letter allows her to put into words her dreams for this new phase of her life. It helps her to see that her youngest child will soon be at school, that she is now close enough to try to heal an old rift with her parents, and that her husband is much happier and freer to be back home. She realizes that she wants and needs to make time for herself to spend time on the writing that is her passion. She finishes her letter:

'By the way, you lucky cow, how do you find time to keep fit in all of this? You realize not everyone gets to live in paradise while they're getting on with life.'

A gentle reminder that the move back to Australia was a good one.

Looking to the future is a hopeful thing to do. By writing yourself a letter from the future you are encouraging yourself to make quite explicit the hopes and dreams that you carry around inside you. Once you have set them down on paper they are harder to ignore. Of course, your wishes, your dreams, your desires may change, but by writing down your hopes you breathe life into them, you move yourself closer to realizing them.

Once again there is nothing new in this.

Dreams on their own are not enough, but they are a starting point. Your dreams are the vision, then you need to make a plan and start building.

Peggy is 29 years old and works as operations manager for a small cosmetics company. Over the next two years she wants to focus on her career, developing the strategic side of her job and moving away from more mundane tasks. In her letter from the future she describes having just run a marathon. She talks about her new job as the e-commerce manager, the Open University Management Diploma she has just completed, and how she has finally conquered her fear of public speaking. She describes how she feels more focused than she has in years and is thinking of applying to study for an MBA. She finishes the letter:

'Company director by the time I'm 35? By then of course I'll be looking more seriously at emigrating to Canada, so I guess I should think about Canadian purchasing accreditation now to show my long-standing commitment.'

Peggy may not achieve everything she dreams of but the letter is an excellent basis for forming a clear and precise plan. She doesn't have to stick rigidly to the plan. Using self-coaching techniques she can adjust her plan as she goes along. The letter is a starting point.

Why a letter?

You could just sit down and think about what you want, imagine yourself living the life you would like. But for it to be real, for it to be useful, you need to engage your emotions. It seems that there is something quite special about writing it down that allows you to reach into your deepest self. Writing about traumatic events in your life makes you healthier, it actually boosts your immune system.[8]

Pete is 42. He works as a lawyer but wants to change the balance of his life so he works less and has more time for other parts of his life. He is teetering on the brink of making some big changes in his life but is not completely sure of the direction he wants to go in. In his letter he describes how he has left fee-earning work and set himself up as a professional support lawyer.

'The law as a business rather than a fee-earning treadmill' is how he puts it. He has set up an office at home and is working part-time, but earning more than before. This leaves him more time for his family and for his other passion – playing drums and percussion. He is working towards his long-term goal of using music and the arts in training. He finishes his letter:

'I hope you get a picture from this letter of what you are becoming. I would not want to deceive by claiming that it has always been easy getting this far. Sometimes I have got stuck, but, as you have already begun to sense, the road levels out as you go on, and you get better at finding refreshment on the route. It is worth it – come on, what is there to lose?'

Tom is 41, lives in London and has a new partner. Both he and his partner, Caro, were married before, although Tom has been single for some time now. He has no children from his first marriage, but Caro has two. They are now expecting their first child together and so are facing some big changes. Their situation is quite complex as there are lots of people involved, including the three children and Caro's former husband.

In Tom's letter from the future he describes how delighted he is with his little daughter, how his relationship with Caro has strengthened and deepened, and how the other children have adapted well. He writes from their new home in the country. He has moved from television production into writing, taken up furniture design in his spare time and has got back into his music.

He also uses the letter to explore a very painful recent event in his life.

'Ann dying in 1998 still eats away. There have been periodic cathartic times of special grief, but usually I feel a dull, sad ache that I know will never leave me – nor do I want it to. Yes, I can remember the joy of a sister who we always said was a twin separated by five years, but her death is still a bewildering absence. Those two years without seeing her daughter were awful, too. Now I've seen her and established more of a regular contact, it's kept me in touch with Ann in a new way. She would never have wanted me to be absent from Grace for anything like as long as I was.'

The letter from the future is for you. You can use it to explore any aspect of your life you like. You need never show it to anyone else. The closer to your real feelings you can get, the more useful you will find this exercise.

You are never too old to write yourself a letter from the future. Here is one written by Alice, who is 90. For five years she has been working on a book about an early feminist writer. Several publishers have shown an interest but none has taken it up. Now suddenly she has heard that one wants to go ahead and publish the book. She is very excited at the prospect. She has been a teacher and journalist all her life but this is the first full-length book she has produced. Here she imagines what might happen to it.

'The book sits proudly among the last papers and material. There it is, the outward and visible sign of the long journey from its first form. Dreams really. In a few minutes I must be off to the TV studio to join a panel of writers whose work on women's achievements has been published recently. It has pleased me enormously that the book has been translated into Spanish and the French edition has already come out. I am to fly to Paris next week for the presentation. Also, and perhaps most importantly, a French Peruvian co-production team want to see the work, with a view to making a film. Books, film, travel, all coming together, typical of these years and what my dreams and activities are all about.'

Just having these visions of the future of the book will help her to push it through the final stages of preparation for publication.

Understanding values

In order to work out what it is you really want, what you really need from your life, you need to work out what your values are. Values and beliefs have always been powerful motivating factors in our lives, so much so that throughout history people have been prepared to die for them. We all live life by some kind of value. Commonly listed ones are security, challenge, job satisfaction, family life and health. We need to make our values explicit to ourselves so that we can be in control and to make real decisions about our lives.

We need to make our values explicit to ourselves.

Below is a list of values. Some of these might be important to you. Perhaps all of them. Perhaps you have other values that you would need to add.

Accomplishment	Freedom to choose	Nurturing
Accuracy	Giving	Order
Adventure	Growth	Participation
Authenticity	Harmony	Peace
Collaboration	Honesty	Personal Power
Community	Humour	Recognition
Comradeship	Independence	Reward
Courage	Integrity	Respect
Creativity	Interdependence	Self-actualization
Empowerment	Joy	Spirituality
Excellence	Lightness	Success
Focus	Love	Zest

The fact is, most of us rarely sit down and actually work out what is important to us. We forget what really matters and carry on fighting the little battles that don't really matter. Once again it is a case of reminding ourselves what we care about, taking the time to sit back and look at our lives and adjust the direction in which we are travelling so that it fits better with what we believe is important.

'After the divorce life seemed so difficult and complicated. At times I felt like I just couldn't cope. Work was making huge demands of me, the children were upset and needed lots of my time and attention. My ex-husband was very angry and bitter and seemed to keep attacking the way I tried to do everything. I was worried about getting older, ending up alone, the house was a mess. Life was chaotic. I knew I had to do something. A friend suggested I sit down and work out what was really important to me and focus on those things. So I made a list. Two things came out top. Keeping the job going and making sure the children were happy. Everything else could wait. I realized I needed some peace and order in my life.

I decided to delegate everything else, or just let it go. I found someone to come in to do the housework, the shopping, everything. I stopped going out in the evenings. I spent all the money I earned on keeping the house going but I knew that that was all that mattered. It's been very difficult but by focusing so much of my attention on the children I stopped feeling so guilty about what had happened to them and by really applying myself at work things started to go really well there, which gave me a great deal of satisfaction.

In some ways my life seems simpler now. I have a few friends who are important to me and I try to see them, but most nights I eat with the children and go to bed early. As for my sex life, well that is non-existent. But you know what, at the moment that just doesn't matter to me. The children are settling down, I am calmer, and as for a new relationship, well, that will happen when it does.'

Kate, 38, single mother, television producer

Working out what your values are gives you a kind of freedom. Once you know what is important to you you can give up wasting your time on things, people or activities that don't mean much to you and spend that time instead on the things you really care about. We so often find ourselves doing things because we think we ought to or because it is what other people want for us.

Howard had been brought up to work hard. He left school at 16 and trained to be an electrician. At 20 he studied to become an electrical contractor. Now he was licensed to employ other people. All through this time, through his studies and his work, he had a feeling of heaviness. He was succeeding and achieving, but something didn't seem quite right. He had thought he would open his own electrical business in the town where he lived and worked. But this vision, although it seemed worthy, didn't hold any joy for him. Dissatisfied, he applied for and got a job overseas. He went away and worked for three years as an electrician in heavy industry. Still he wasn't satisfied. Finally he realized that what he loved was studying, reading, researching ideas and theories. He just loved using his mind to solve complex problems.

'When I realized that what I really wanted to do was study it was like rocks falling off my shoulders. I had been working myself towards a future I just didn't want. Straight away I left my job, booked my ticket back home and applied to university. A world that had seemed completely closed to me suddenly opened up in front of me. Really I've never looked back.'

Howard, 32, research scientist

It is not easy to work out what your values are, what the important things in your life are, and like everything else these change.

Angela's story

Just occasionally you meet someone who has made a really big change in their lives, someone who has not given up on their dreams but has managed to live them instead.

Angela became a professional actress at the age of 50. She managed to break into an overcrowded, insecure, uncertain profession, long after most people would have even thought of it. At 49 she auditioned for the Royal Academy of Dramatic Art (RADA), and with a little help from friends and acquaintances she had her first professional job at 50. She went on to have a successful career on stage and television, appearing in London's West End with Alan Alda.

'As far back as I can remember I knew acting was what I wanted to do and I can remember my mother saying, "If we had the money darling, I'd send you to RADA". But it never got any further than that.

I left school at 15 and helped in the pub and all that, but in my heart of hearts I knew that acting was what I wanted to do. But I'd already almost realized that it simply wasn't going to happen and life went on and I didn't do anything about it. And then I eventually got married and had children.

I filled the need to act by doing a lot of amateur work. There was a very good amateur theatre where we lived and we did put on some damn good shows and I'm very proud of a lot of the things we did.

Then suddenly it dawned on me. The children were ready to leave home. I remember thinking "My God, I can now do whatever I like more or less."

I remember lying in bed almost pounding the pillow thinking, "What am I going to do about this? Because this lovely little theatre group I'm with simply isn't enough, it really isn't. But what can I do? How can I make the jump?" And this was at the time when you couldn't get an equity card unless you'd done professional work and you couldn't do professional work unless you had a card. It was that awful catch 22. So I was talking to a friend of mine who was also in the amateur theatre group and she said, "Why don't you go and audition for RADA and do the course? And then you could teach." People often think that teaching will fill the gap, she was a teacher, maybe that influenced her.

But I did think actually going to RADA might be a good idea, doing the audition, because at least that way I could talk to people on the inside of the profession. In other words if someone there said, "Yes, I think you are good enough to try," then that would be like everything I could wish for.

So I telephoned RADA and found that they will audition anyone. If you paid your fee then you could be auditioned. So they sent me the form and I filled it in. And then one day the phone rang and they said, "We've had a cancellation, you can come on Monday."

And I was so shocked because I'd sort of thought, "Oh, I'll think about it in a little while, I'll think about some pieces," because I knew I had to do have two pieces ready and then all of a sudden I thought, "Oh my god what have I done? I must be mad."

I was well aware that I would probably be the only one of my age, I did realize that there can't be many 49-year-old women applying to RADA. Whether that was why they decided to bung me in early or not I don't know.

I was terrified about being older. I remember saying to my husband, "Oh look, this is silly." I suddenly thought, "What are you doing? They're going to see all these 18-year-olds. What are they going to do with you?" And I began to have all these terrible doubts and it was my dear husband who said, "For goodness sake go, you never know what you might miss. Go.'"

Buoyed up by her audition at RADA, and with help from Miriam Karlin (a well-known and successful British actress) and others, Angela persisted in her aim to get a professional acting job. Eventually, after a year of letters and calls, she auditioned for a part in Ibson's *Hedda Gabler* at Theatre Clwydd, a successful professional theatre in Wales.

'Some months later I was at the kitchen sink peeling the potatoes and the phone rang and this man's voice said, "I am Patrick someone of Theatre Clwydd, Annie wants you to play Aunt Julie in *Hedda Gabler*." Honestly, when I tell you now it makes me cry because of all the emotions. Standing at the kitchen sink and to hear that she wanted me to be in the play. After that job I managed to get an agent and since then I've had all the ups and downs that any jobbing actor has.

I sometimes look back at my life and I can see it scattered with mistakes, and wrong turnings and silly decisions and you know things you should have got right and didn't and my life has certainly been overflowing with those, but I do sometimes think, "But I got that right." There are some things, I look at my boys and I think well, "that wasn't too bad," and I look at that and it's sort of carried me through other things.'

When we asked Angela what it was that pushed her to make the leap when so many people don't, she said: 'I only know that I'd got to the stage where I simply had to do it. It was more than a desire, it was a need.'

Perhaps to make real changes in our lives we have to learn how to turn our wants, our desires, into needs. Because then we can do anything.

'Power exists – as it always has – in providing people with dreams.'
                                                                    Funky Business[9]

Try completing this sentence:

'If everything in my life had gone as well as it could have, by now I'd be …'

Then ask yourself:

Which part of my life is not being fulfilled that I think would be fulfilled if I had achieved this? What can I do about it now?

STEP FOUR

Creating Dreams

Task: write yourself a letter from the future.

Task: identify the main values in your life.

05

chapter five
whatever turns you on
exploring motivation

> 'Ours is a world where people don't know what they want and
> are willing to go through hell to get it.'   Don Marquis, 1878–1937

What do you really want?

Beyond the basic needs of food, warmth and shelter, no one can
really know exactly what it is that drives each individual. The
complex drives and desires that fuel behaviour are a source of
speculation and research. Much has been written on the subject of
motivation. Theories abound. But there are some things we can be
sure of:

◆ Different things motivate different people.

◆ Any one person is motivated by different factors at different
  times.

◆ We often don't understand exactly what it is that motivates us to
  act.

One area where there is evidence that the use of psychological
techniques can foster change and enhance performance is sport.[1] But
even here it is not clear what actually motivates people to take part
in sport, or to have the determination to succeed. We might assume
that winning is a big motivating factor for anyone taking part in
sport, but plenty of people run marathons with no hope of actually
winning. The fact is they have set themselves some kind of inner
goal, even if it is just to finish the course, and it is this goal that
motivates them to continue.

What does the research show?

Looking into the motives athletes cite for their participation in sport, research[2] conducted in Britain and America reveals the following. The pattern of motives did not vary significantly between the sexes, or across age groups or cultures.

Very important motives	Moderately important motives
Personal improvement	Exhilaration and excitement
Health and fitness	Feelings of personal control
Making friends	**Relatively unimportant motives**
Fun	To intimidate or control others
Winning	Medals, trophies, etc.

We tend to think of sport in terms of winning and losing, but like most other things in life it is much more complicated.

'The moment of victory is much too short to live for that and nothing else.'
Martina Navratilova, tennis champion

Sport seems to appeal to our most fundamental human make-up. It has an attraction that exists across cultures and throughout time. The Ancient Egyptians, the Ancient Greeks, the people of Mesopotamia, all played sport. Pre-contact Aboriginals in Australia played a range of sports, using balls, sticks and boomerangs. In every walk of life people create games and sports.

Sports psychologists have long understood that there is a strong link between body and mind. Perhaps it is not always the athlete who is best in terms of skills and talent that wins, but the one who has the best mental attitude.

'I coached the twins and they were both very good. But I always knew that Luke would be the one to make it. Physically they were the same. Their ability was the same, but Luke had a need to win, a determination, a belief in himself that Sam just hadn't got.' Paul, coach for Luke and Sam, identical twins and 1500 metre runners

Studies show that great achievers in every field often create dreams or visions of exactly what they want to do and how they are going to get it. In fact, research from Manchester University shows that physical strength can be increased by just thinking about an exercise.

What does the research show?

Researchers at Manchester Metropolitan University measured the push that 18 male volunteers could exert with their little fingers.[3] Six of the group were asked to repeat the exercise twice a week for a month. Another six had to imagine doing the workouts but not actually do them. The rest were asked to do nothing at all. Four weeks later, when the volunteers were tested again, the researchers found that the average strength of the physical-practice group had increased by 33 per cent, and that of the mental-practice group by 16 per cent. The group that did nothing stayed roughly the same. Researchers think that the imagined exercise initiates the same motor programme in the brain as real exercise, and improves the neural pathways. The study suggests that mental practice could help build strength in athletes and speed up patients' rehabilitation following brain injuries.

We don't really know how our brains work, but some people aren't waiting for science to tell them, they already know the power of visualization. Many sports men and women know that mental imagery is an effective way of improving performance.

'I never hit a shot, even in practice, without having a sharp, in-focus picture of it in my head. It's like a colour movie. First, I "see" the ball where I want it to finish, nice and white and sitting up high on the bright green grass. Then the scene quickly changes, and I "see" the ball going there: its path, trajectory and shape, even its behaviour on landing. Then there's a sort of fade-out, and the next scene shows me making the kind of swing that will turn the previous images into reality. Only at the end of this short, private Hollywood spectacular do I select a club and step up to the ball.'

Jack Nicklaus, golfing champion

And it goes beyond sport into business. Even traditional industrial firms admit that emotion and imagination are the way forward.

Discomfort is your friend

The comfortzone is made up of the familiar – the things, thoughts, feelings and behaviours that we are used to. It's comfortable staying with the familiar, and it's often uncomfortable to change. But on the other hand change is what we want. So we have to move into the discomfort zone. This is the zone of possibilities. This is where the change is. So feelings of discomfort as we begin a new change programme are good signs that we are moving forward – discomfort really is our friend when we want to make real change.

What motivates us to change?

Sport is all very well and it is an interesting area to look at, but sport is not life. The rules of life are much more complex and when we try to change something about the way we live we find ourselves facing conflicting emotions. It often seems easier to do nothing and stay in the comfort zone. The fact is, most people don't really understand the process of change. That's why their attempts to change a behaviour are often unsuccessful. Some people think of change as being a simple decision to do something different. In reality it is a far more complex process.

Some people think of change as being a simple decision to do something different.

- ◆ Motivated, directed change is a complex, ongoing process.

- ◆ The intensity of our motivation fluctuates considerably from one time or situation to the other.

- ◆ The most enduring characteristic of change is ambivalence, the simultaneous existence of two conflicting ideas.

- ◆ Ambivalence is normal. It is OK and normal to have mixed feelings about change.

- ◆ You don't have to be 100 per cent committed, 51 per cent is enough.

It is important to recognize that 'relapse' is a normal and common part of the change process and to not give up.

There is, however, a paradox here. Sometimes if we have too clear a vision of where we want to get to we use up all our energy being fixed on the future and we have nothing left for now. We become stifled by a rigid view of the future. There is no time or energy left for now.

'Soon as I got in the pool, I thought, "Right this is it." As soon as I got in the water, my stroke was flowing and I felt great. And down the first 50 – as soon as that – I went. "Oh my God I'm winning, I'm going to win!" and I just lost it.'

Susan Jackson, Mihalyi Csikszentmihalyi, *Flow in Sports.*

In order to be happy and effective it seems we have to feel that we are moving towards something worthwhile. Our life has to be informed by a bigger view. But at the same time we must not lose sight of the fact that now is all we have. It is a sort of paradox, but then, who said it was going to be easy? A fulfilling life is something we have to work hard for.

'If we take eternity to mean not infinite temporal duration but timelessness, then eternal life belongs to those who live in the present. Our life has no end in just the way in which our visual field has no limits.'

Ludwig Wittgenstein, 6.4311 *Tractatus Logico-Philosophicus*

Creating motivation

Motivation doesn't really exist outside of action. If you wait around to be motivated before you take action you may well never begin anything at all. The word motivation comes from the Latin and means 'movement'. Motivation is movement. By taking action, by setting out along the path, we start the process, we create our own motivation. Ironically, it is often this first step, this beginning, which is the most difficult.

'Taking a new step, uttering a new word is what people fear most.'
Fyodor Dostoevsky

Something to aim for

One way to get started along the path is to create a goal. Give yourself something to aim for.

'I decided I needed to get fit so I joined a gym. Part of my programme was five minutes on the running machine. I had never done it before and I thought it sounded pretty boring but I did it because they put it on my chart. Then I noticed there was a challenge at the gym to get you to see if you could run a half marathon over the space of a month. You had to fill in your time on the graph on the wall. I thought it was a good idea. I liked the thought of being able to run a half marathon, even if it did take a month to do it.

I was telling some friends about it and one of them mentioned a 10k charity run that she was doing. She said they were looking for more people. I sent off for the form and decided to go in for it. I started training in the park. Other friends heard about it and about four of them said they wanted to do it too. There were five of us in the end. We had six weeks to train. We got quite serious about it.

The day of the race came. There were about 8,000 people taking part. It was a fantastic feeling. It was a cancer charity and lots of people had the names of friends or relatives pinned to their T-shirts. You know, running in memory of, or running in celebration of. It was very moving.

Between us we raised about £1,000. Quite amazing, all from nothing really, just an idea. We have all kept up the running, we go once a week now. I will definitely do the race next year and I know there are other friends who are interested in doing it too.

The sense of achievement was incredible. I had never thought of doing anything like that before. I never thought of myself as "a runner". In fact, at school I hated running. The whole thing just gathered momentum and I feel so much fitter than I did before.'

Jackie, 33, management accountant

Motivation is a process

Motivation is not a product. We can measure motivation only by the way it affects our behaviour. If we are motivated, we act. If someone were to say to you that they were very motivated to get fit but did nothing at all about it, you would seriously doubt their motivation. Motivation and action are one. So by taking action you can start a process and create motivation.

Goals in themselves do not create motivation.

Goals in themselves do not create motivation, but they give us a direction in which to travel. If you are motivated, a specific goal will give you a target to head for, a focus for your activities, but it will not in itself create motivation; only action can do this.

Research carried out in the USA with tens of thousands of subjects over the course of 30 years has shown that if we have a goal to aim for we are more likely to be successful.

What does the research show?

In 1996 Edwin Locke at the University of Maryland reviewed 30 years of research into the relationship between goal setting and performance on work tasks.[5] More than 40,000 people took part in these studies. The participants ranged from children to research scientists. The studies took place in eight countries, with time spans of between 1 minute and 24 years, and were both laboratory and field studies. These were just some of the findings:

▶

- ◆ The more difficult the goal, the greater the achievement.

- ◆ The more specific or explicit the goal the more precisely the performance is regulated.

- ◆ Goals that are both specific and difficult lead to the highest performance.

- ◆ Commitment to goals is most critical when goals are specific and difficult.

- ◆ High commitment to goals is attained when:

  a) the individual is convinced that the goal is important;

  b) the individual is convinced that the goal is attainable (or at least that progress can be made towards it).

- ◆ Goal setting is most effective when there is feedback showing progress in relation to the goal.

- ◆ Goal setting mediates the effect of knowledge of past performance on subsequent performance.

- ◆ Goals stimulate planning.

The more difficult the goal, the more we achieve. Sir Edmund Hillary again:

'I would advise them [young people] to aim high. To set their sights at a pretty tough target and don't be too worried if you're not successful at first. Just keep persisting and keep improving your standards and ultimately you've got a pretty fair chance at achieving your desired goal.'   Sir Edmund Hillary

For goals to be useful they need to be specific, otherwise it is difficult to measure whether or not we are achieving them. There is a conflict here, however. Because if goals are too specific they can become stifling; if we are too fixated on the end point, we lose energy for the journey. We need a broad vision of the future which we can use to develop specific goals

Setting goals

One of the qualities of being human is that we can imagine the future. This is not always to our advantage. Fear of the future and fear of change can often hold us back. Of course, we can imagine what we would really like and strive to get it, but we can also imagine ourselves failing, we can see the humiliation and defeat before us.

Nevertheless, to some extent the future is in our control. By setting ourselves goals we can work towards achieving the things we want. But however well we plan our lives, we cannot totally control all the events that surround us, however much some people would like to try.

What we can do is learn to deal with what happens to us, to apply our life values to every situation we find ourselves in. This is why it is so important to find out what really matters to us, what it is we are really striving for.

'Everything can be taken away from man but one thing – to choose one's own attitude in a given set of circumstances, to choose one's own way.'
Viktor Frankl, psychiatrist, Auschwitz survivor

So we cannot necessarily choose what happens to us, but we can choose the way we view it. However, if you want to change any aspect of your life, and feel more fulfilled, you have to work out what it is you want. You can't hit a target that you don't have, or reach a goal that doesn't exist.

All change involves ambiguous feeling.

All change involves ambiguous feeling. There will always be reasons for staying in the comfort zone, for preserving the status quo and leaving things as they are. Except of course we can never really leave things as they are. Life is about change. Seasons change, we grow older, friends move away, the company relocates, our skills become outdated. No matter what we do, things change. We feel that by doing nothing we leave things as they are, but of course this is not true.

'No one keeps his enthusiasm automatically. Enthusiasm must be nourished with new actions, new aspirations, new efforts, new vision.'
Papyrus

Then again, we don't want to take responsibility. If we don't make any decisions, don't choose any course of action, then nothing can be our fault. The sad thing is that if we never cause anything to happen, as well as never failing, we can never succeed, or at least we can never take the credit for our successes.

So we may not fully or even partially understand motivation, but research has shown that there are ways of increasing motivation. In fact, we can create our own motivation. One key to doing this is to set goals.

Goals must be SMART

This means that when we set goals we need to be SMART:

- **S** **specific** – vague goals lead to vague, half-hearted attempts to achieve them.
- **M** **measurable** – we need to be able to evaluate our progress.
- **A** **attractive** – if we don't want it, we're unlikely to put in a sustained effort.
- **R** **realistic** – we must be capable of achieving the goal.
- **T** **time-framed** – we need to have an appropriate time frame in mind.

It also means that we need to distinguish between a vision and a goal.

Vision vs Goals

Good broad vision but poor goal	Good specific goal
◆ Feel fit and healthy and good about my body.	◆ Join a gym, exercise three times a week, eat a healthy diet, take 'time out' for myself.
◆ Be financially independent.	◆ Have my own business up and running within two years.

Tom is feeling stressed. He finds his job stimulating and rewarding, but very demanding. He also has a young family and his partner works part-time. He is finding he has to work longer and longer hours to get the work done. He is beginning to feel that he is losing touch with his two daughters, aged three and five. One of the children is developing a stammer and Tom and his wife have been advised that she may need more one-to-one attention.

He decides to develop a SMART goal to deal with the situation. His overall aim is to spend more time with his daughters and to feel less stressed. Here is his goal:

S Spend one hour each week exclusively with each child, letting the child choose the activity.

M Arrive home from work before 6.30pm three evenings a week.

A He hopes his daughter's speech will improve if he spends more time with her.

R Not sure that he can make it three evenings but he will try.

T He will try this for one month and then review his progress.

▶

After one month he realizes that it is just not feasible to get home before 6.30pm three evenings a week. Tom cuts this down to two evenings. He informs his colleagues that he has to leave the office by 5.30 on Wednesdays and Fridays. He finds that the hour session with each child works better as two half-hour slots. This is of course not the only time he spends with them, but he does find that the 'special time' spent with each child makes a huge difference to his relationship with them.

He also goes to the library and reads up about stammering.

Tom's overall vision is of a happy balance, a fulfilled life, one in which his children are happy and thriving. But to turn his vision into reality he needs these very clear, specific, measurable goals.

Rachel is 36 years old. She is married but has no children and lives in a smart flat in a fashionable quarter of a big city. She went to work in the marketing department of a small computer consultancy at 18 and had been there ever since, surviving mergers and buyouts. She is bright and has worked her way up to head of department on a good salary.

However, something in her was not fulfilled. She knew she wanted more. Materially her life was very comfortable, but she began to feel she needed more of a challenge. She also began to feel she would like more freedom to choose the hours she worked. She wrote herself a SMART goal.

S To run my own successful business.

M In two years' time I want to be making at least as much money as I am earning now.

A I want to start off working from home, I don't want to spend more hours on the business than I do at work.

R It must be something that I have the expertise to do now. I must put aside some start-up money and not use more than that. It must be money that I have saved and can afford to lose.

T If I have not recovered my initial investment within one year I will give up.

She started to look around for something she could do. She saw a small cleaning firm being advertised for sale and decided to buy it with the money she had saved. It was a risk, but one she was prepared to take. She had considerable business and marketing experience and by keeping her overheads low, recruiting good staff, and with clever sales and marketing, she managed to turn the company round. Within three years it was a highly successful business with a turnover that wildly exceeded her expectations. Rachel was nominated for a 'Business Woman of the Year' award, presented by a national newspaper. She won.

When asked about the key to her success, Rachel said:

'I took calculated risks and worked hard. I knew how much money I was prepared to lose and I had a fall-back plan. I knew that if it didn't work I had enough experience to go back to the kind of work I was doing before. I saw it as an adventure, as fun, I didn't take it too seriously, and I knew that if I failed I would survive.'

Maintaining motivation

A key to maintaining your motivation is to see that you are moving in the direction you want to go and that you are gaining benefit for your efforts. To do this you need to be able to measure your success. If your actions bring you closer to your goal, if you can see that what you are doing really works, then your motivation will increase. If you understand that change is difficult and that in any change process you will not feel motivated all the time, you will be able to work with the degree of motivation you feel.

If you use self-coaching techniques to keep checking that you are moving towards your goals and that the goals you are moving towards are the ones you believe in or wish to achieve, your motivation will just naturally keep growing.

Dealing with procrastination – procrastinate later

Procrastination is an extremely common problem. More than 20 per cent of adults consider themselves to be chronic procrastinators[6] – and the other procrastinators didn't get around to filling out the questionnaires. It has been estimated that there are six styles of procrastination: the perfectionist, the dreamer, the worrier, the defier, the crisis-maker and the over-doer.[7] If you are a procrastinator you can probably identify quite easily which is your main style.

Regardless of your individual procrastination style, it's possible to overcome procrastination. The first step is to accept that you have been a procrastinator in the past, but now you're fed up with the difficulties this has brought into your life.

You might like to make a list, mental or written, of the problems that procrastination has caused you, and another list of how much more comfortable your life would be if you broke the routine of procrastination. In this way you can consciously work on changing the balance of the costs and benefits of change and by doing this you can move yourself out of the contemplation stage (which is where procrastination is) into the action stage.

When you feel procrastination rear its ugly head you might like to ask yourself the following question:[8]

◆ How do I *feel* about the task that I'm putting off now?

◆ What are the *advantages* of starting this right now?

◆ What are the *disadvantages* of leaving it until later?

◆ What *excuses* am I making for not doing this task right now?

◆ Will it *kill me* to do it for a few minutes at a time?

◆ How can I *break the task down* into manageable sections?

◆ What *reward* can I give myself for finishing it?

Maximize your motivation

Task: for each of the life areas you identified in Chapter 2 write down the positive and negative impact of making changes.

Task: for each life area set yourself a SMART goal.

chapter six
from negative to positive
turning ANTs into PETs

Fear of failure

'Every time you win, it diminishes the fear a little bit. You never really cancel the fear of losing; you keep challenging it.'

Arthur Ashe, 1943–1993, US tennis player, AIDS spokesperson

Most of us are prone to negative beliefs about ourselves at some time during our lives. If we can identify these negative thoughts and beliefs we can change them into positive thoughts. If we change our thoughts and beliefs, we can begin to change our behaviour.

Many people hold negative beliefs about themselves. Beliefs like these:

'If someone criticizes me then there must be something wrong with me.'

'I am basically inferior to other people even if they don't see it.'

'I must have love and approval in order to feel good about myself.'

We somehow manage to be our own harshest critics. We forget all the good things we have done, everything we have achieved, and focus on shortcomings and failures. Part of this is that we tend to enjoy the things we are good at and if we enjoy them they can seem easy. They cause us little or no pain, so we pay no attention to them. If your shoes are a comfortable fit you forget about them. You become aware only if they are tight and pinching or if there is a stone in one of them. The negative things in our lives have a habit of demanding all our attention.

'Well, I suppose I do have a small talent, in a particular area. I suppose I am good at leading my team. My staff trust me and I always get the job done. If the pressure's really on and I need people to stay late and work weekends, they'll do it for me. They know that I won't ask them unless it's completely necessary.

Yes I suppose that is a skill of a kind, getting people to do the work.' Rafael, 34, creative director

This man heads up a successful department. He is known, liked and trusted by many people. He is superbly good at his job, but he can hardly give himself credit. And this is not false modesty – he really believes that he has just a small talent in a particular area and that anyone could do what he does. In fact, he has fantastic leadership and communication skills and his staff are devoted and loyal. These skills come to him easily and so he discounts them or is simply not aware of them.

We are all prone to doubts and fears about our own abilities.

We are all prone to doubts and fears about our own abilities. At some time in our lives we all feel that we are not as good as we would like to be, or could be.

Feelings are real, but they are not reality

In our Western society we tend to treat our feelings as though they represent reality. If we are afraid of something, we believe that whatever it is we are afraid of is in fact dangerous or frightening. But our feelings are not reality, and feelings can and do change.

For example, it is common to feel anxious and nervous before going on a long journey. This does not mean that we shouldn't go, it just means we feel nervous.

'Mum and I sat on the plane and looked at each other. I said to her, "What on earth are we doing? Why are we going?" We were on our way to Cuba, a place I had dreamed of going for as long as I could remember. Mum's family is from there originally and we had always wanted to go and visit. Now I could think of nothing else I would rather do, if I could have got off the plane at that moment I would have done. I was quite simply terrified. Of the heat, the poverty, the corruption, the fact that I hardly spoke the language, everything. I imagined being kidnapped, hijacked, everything.

But of course I didn't get off. As soon as we arrived I felt better and by the next day I was tired but completely fine. We had a great holiday, met all sorts of long-lost relatives, and I think I had the most fantastic two weeks of my life. My fears before we left were just that, fears. They had nothing to do with reality. I was just afraid to go to a country that I knew so little about and that I had never been to before.

Marina, 22, journalist

Everyone knows the two o'clock in the morning syndrome. In the middle of the night anxieties and worries increase. A problem that seems manageable during the daytime can seem completely overpowering in the middle of the night. Then the morning comes and we feel better. Nothing has changed except the daylight and our feelings.

Negative self-talk and false assumptions – giving our power away

There are powerful interactions between our thoughts, feelings and behaviour. Changing our behaviour affects our feelings and thoughts and changing our thoughts will affect our behaviour.

Phobias are a good example of the relationship between thoughts, feelings and behaviour. People with agoraphobia have an intense fear of going out into open spaces, shopping centres or public places where they can't escape. If they push themselves to go out, often they have panic attacks. Their heart pounds, they start to feel as if they can't catch their breath, they have chest pains and often get frightened that they are about to die. Not surprisingly they rush off home or to a place they feel safe as quickly as they can.

'I won't be able to cope with this situation.'
'I'll panic and it will be absolutely terrible.'
'I can't stand the way I feel.'
'I'm going to have a heart attack and die.'

Their automatic negative thoughts run away with them. In an attempt to prepare for the worst their attention gets more and more focused on their body and any small changes are interpreted as warning signs. They become increasingly panic struck. Over time they avoid possible fear-inducing situations. They never stay around long enough to learn that it is really quite safe to be out in the open.

Usually fear warns us of a danger and is there to protect us, but in the case of a phobic the fear exists irrespective of the reality of the danger. The feeling of fear is real, but the danger is not. They have given away their power.

When we start something new and challenging, and as we move out of our comfort zone, we often begin to feel anxious about what we are doing. We may get caught up in a cycle of negative self-talk.

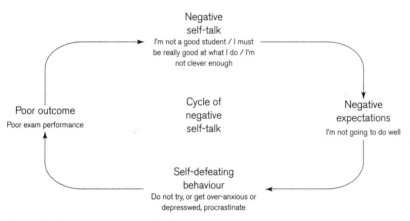

Figure 6.1 Cycle of negative self-talk

Let's examine these negative thoughts. Figure 6.1 charts the cycle of negative talk of a college student about to take exams.

So what can you do about these negative thoughts? The answer is you have to consciously and deliberately change them into positive ones. This means examining where they come from and challenging them. There is no point just saying to yourself:

'I am a good student.'

'I am clever enough'

if you don't actually believe it. You need to examine some of your negative thoughts and find ways of disputing them.

'There is nothing either good or bad, but thinking makes it so.'

Hamlet

The ABCDE model

The ABCDE model[1] reminds us that it is what we think that determines what we feel, and that we can exert a good deal of influence over our thoughts and in this way change how we feel.

Where does negative self talk come from?

Humans are highly complex beings. Our bodies are in a constant state of change: there are literally millions of things that need to be done just to keep our bodies alive and functioning. We don't even think about most of the physical things we do just to keep ourselves up and about. At a conscious level we are hardly aware of breathing, regulating our temperature, putting one foot in front of the other to walk about. Just as our bodies have many automatic forms of behaviour, our minds have developed many automatic beliefs. Some of these are negative and limiting. We usually don't talk about our negative thoughts, and we usually don't question them or purposefully try to change them. This is because they are so much a part of us that we are hardly aware of them. Yet ironically they exert a powerful influence on our behaviour.

Negative self-talk may have built up over years.

Negative self-talk may have built up over years. Every time we have failed at something, been criticized, felt stupid, we have added to our negative self-talk. It is impossible to know where it has all come from, but if we can recognize and identify it there are ways of disputing and so changing it.

'Keep away from people who try to belittle your ambitions. Small people always do that, but the really great make you feel that you too can become great.'

Mark Twain

At the highest level of consciousness are the things that we are aware we say to ourselves:

'I'm good at tennis.'

'I always lose at chess.'

At the next level is automatic self-talk. At this level we are normally not aware of what it is that we are saying to ourselves, but quite often these automatic thoughts pop up. We can also train ourselves to become more aware of these thoughts.

An example of this level of thought might be preparing to give a presentation to your boss or an important client and feeling rather anxious about the outcome. You may have brief moments of awareness of your automatic self-talk which may say things like:

'I'll never get this right. I always get so nervous.'

We don't have just one automatic self-talk thought about a situation. There are a whole series of them, linked together. The thought:

'I'll never get this right. I always get so nervous.'

could be linked to the thought:

'I'm just not good/clever enough to do this well.'

This in turn might be linked to the thought:

'I've never done well enough, I feel a failure.'

or

'No one ever thinks I'm any good.'

and so on …

The next level is the deep underlying beliefs that we have about ourselves and the world. These are normally subconscious. They are powerful core beliefs, often expressed as quite simple statements about ourselves and the world. In a way they represent our world view, that is, our basic perspective on life. An example of these, in relation to the previous thoughts, might be:

'I am a failure.'

or

'I'm not good enough.'

or

'Life is unfair and hard.'

Self-limiting beliefs

By holding on to our self-limiting beliefs we can make sure that life is stressful and difficult. If we judge others by these standards we can also make sure that we live an isolated and lonely life.

Below are some commonly held self-limiting beliefs.[2] Do you recognize any of them? Do you hold any others?

I can't do things I don't like doing.

If someone criticizes me there must be something wrong with me.

Mistakes are terrible things.

Other people are to blame for my problems.

I am bound to feel depressed for ever because the problems in my life are insoluble.

I must always live up to everyone's expectations.

If I delegate I will completely lose control of the situation.

Life should be easy.

No one asks for my opinion.

You've got to get everything right first time.

No one wants to get to know me.

I must be perfect or people won't accept me. This means:

◆ *I must have a perfect relationship, feel totally in love with my partner and never fight or quarrel with them.*

◆ *I must always be happy and control all my negative emotions.*

◆ *I must not be vulnerable and flawed.*

◆ *I must have a perfect sex life.*

◆ *I must succeed in everything I do.*

◆ *I must not lower or fall short of my moral standards, ever.*

'Don't worry about perfection. You will never achieve it.'

Salvador Dali, 1904–1989, painter

Paradoxically, the thoughts that are not in our immediate awareness are the ones that exert the greatest and most consistent influence on our behaviour. Imagine having someone sitting on your shoulder whispering into your ear:

'You can't do this, you don't deserve to do well, you're pathetic.'

It is not helpful in terms of our performance. We need encouragement not discouragement.

The urge to over-control

The urge to over control is very common.[3] People who have a high urge to control tend to be less happy in their lives in general[4] and tend not to be good at working with others.[5] As we know, good leaders are rare. Perhaps you are in charge of a department or team or perhaps it is your job to run a project. If you are overworked or feeling pressure from above you may well feel the urge to over-control your team or your project. You may find yourself with thoughts like these:

'If I don't shout at people, then nothing will get done.'

'I can't rely on people to do it right first time.'

'If I don't stay right on top of them, it's going to be a complete and utter disaster.'

'If this doesn't get done exactly the way I want, it means I am not a good manager.'

The underlying beliefs that are driving you – that provide permission to be over-controlling – are:

'If I absolutely control everything, this project will work out well.'

The underpinning rules of this sort of belief are:

'People must know their place in the hierarchy.'

'You must never challenge my decisions.'

'You must not make decisions for yourself, even though I have delegated responsibility to you.'

It may be that your unconscious self-talk and underlying beliefs are telling you it is the only way to cope. If you took a good look at these beliefs you might find that in fact they are not true and are destructive to the situation. By not acknowledging them you allow yourself to be controlled by unconscious and irrational beliefs.

It may be that even when you are aware of and acknowledge these beliefs you still agree with them. Sometimes and in some situations it is appropriate to exert absolute control just as sometimes it is appropriate to be afraid of spiders, or snakes or birds. But it may be that you are causing yourself a lot of unnecessary stress and anxiety. To be in control of your life you need to free yourself from irrational, unhelpful fears and beliefs.

Cost–benefit analysis

One way of finding out whether or not your beliefs are helpful is to do a cost-benefit analysis. Look at the advantages of holding on to your beliefs and compare these with the disadvantages.

Benefits of believing:

'If I absolutely control everything, this project will work out well.'
'I will stay in control.'
'I won't have to rely on anyone else.'
'Things will be done my way.'
'People will be impressed at my authority.'

Costs of believing:

'I can never relax and trust anyone.'
'I might miss someone else's good ideas.'
'People won't tell me about mistakes.'
'People will talk behind my back.'

Turning ANTs into PETs

We all have powerful subconscious beliefs about ourselves and how we cope with adversity. We are not usually aware of exactly what it is that we believe, but what we think about ourselves and our achievements will have an effect on the way we deal with the problems we encounter during the course of our lives.

There are techniques for dealing with your automatic negative thoughts (ANTs) and turning them into performance-enhancing thoughts (PETs). First you have to identify your negative self-talk. One technique for doing this is laddering. This is how it works.

Laddering

Take some time to think about a problem that you have, one that causes you some worry, anxiety or just simply makes you feel bad. Choose a real-life problem that is causing you some concern or will cause you concern in the very near future.

1. Write down *exactly* what the problem is (be specific, describe the problem in detailed, concrete terms).

2. Now write down the *positive* advantages of solving this problem (once again be specific and write in concrete terms).

3. Now write down the hidden 'benefits' of *not* solving this problem.

4. Now, think about the downside of these benefits: what are the costs of receiving them?

5. Now write down your feelings about the problem: how does this problem make you feel? Really let go and express yourself. Let the feelings out on to the paper. The more you can get in touch with your feelings, the easier it will be to uncover your underlying negative beliefs, and the greater the benefit you will receive from this exercise. You may like to think about, and use, some of the following *feeling* words: *angry, sad, relaxed, guilty, anxious, depressed, hopeless, miserable, serious, frightened, confident, excited, afraid, hopeful, loving, worried, tense, happy, content, overwhelmed, stupid, inferior, ashamed, isolated, withdrawn, self-disgusted, discouraged, useless, tired, defeated, alone, pathetic.*

We now need to work on identifying the self-talk, the thoughts and the beliefs that accompany these feelings using a technique called *laddering*.[6] This is a way of analyzing our automatic self-talk. In laddering we keep looking for more and more basic underlying assumptions, beliefs and thoughts, until we reach our core beliefs; that is, our deep underlying beliefs about ourselves. Once we really know what it is that we think, at this deep level, we can make some powerful changes. This technique is called laddering because it proceeds step by step, like descending a ladder, rung by rung. All we need to do to get at the underlying thought is identify a self-talk statement associated with the problem and the feelings, and ask ourselves:

'What does this mean to me?'

again and again until we get to the underlying belief driving our behaviour.

For example, Lizzie is 26 and has just left her job as a secondary school teacher to go to work for an environmental charity based in a large botanic garden. She was delighted to get the job and loves it although she has been there only three months.

Now her boss Eileen has asked her to accompany her to an international conference on plant conservation. Eileen wants Lizzie to present a paper on education issues in botanic gardens. The conference is taking place in Brazil.

Lizzie is delighted to be asked to go but is very nervous. She has never given a paper at a conference before and is afraid that she will do badly. She is mostly afraid that her nervousness will let her down. She is also worried about holding her own at the rest of the conference. She is not a scientist and she knows most of the other people there are botanists and experts in their fields.

(This is what Lizzie wrote for her laddering exercise.)

1. *Write down exactly what the problem is.*

'I have to go and present a paper at the conference. I am so nervous about getting it wrong that I can hardly work on the paper. The anxiety about this issue is making me do badly in the rest of my work. I am afraid I will be too nervous to do this properly. I wonder whether to say to Eileen that I don't want to do it.'

2. *Now write down the positive advantages of solving this problem*

'If I manage to present the paper and do well, then my self-confidence will be vastly increased. I might really enjoy myself and make some useful contacts for my work. My boss will be really pleased and impressed with me if I do it well. I will feel great about myself. It could be very good for my career, I could put it on my CV.'

Usually when we are indulging in an undesirable behaviour that we can't seem to get rid of, there is almost some kind of pay-off for us in maintaining the behaviour. This pay-off may not be clear to us immediately. For example, not putting 100 per cent effort into studying pays off in that if we do not get good grades, we need not see ourselves as failures. If we never really tried, then we didn't really fail either. Not trying pays off by protecting our self-esteem. If we are to make any real changes, we need to understand the hidden benefits of a problem behaviour.

3. *Now write down the hidden 'benefits' of not solving this problem.*

'If I don't go to the conference I will not have to face my fears. I won't have to work hard on the paper, and I will not have to feel like I am being tested in front of all those people. I can still tell myself that I could have done it if I wanted to without finding out if that is really true. If I go and do the paper badly I can tell myself that I shouldn't have tried, then I won't have to try new things in the future.'

Even though we appear to receive some kind of benefit from not solving the problem, this benefit has its costs too. For example, we may unconsciously protect our self-esteem against failure by never giving 100 per cent, but the cost to us is that we never find out how capable we really are. We can easily go through life never fulfilling our potential, and always under-achieving.

4. *Now, think about the downside of these benefits: what are the costs of receiving them?*

'The main thing is that I will feel bad about myself. My boss will think less of me. I won't get the chance to travel. She may not ask me next time. She may wonder whether I am really up to the job.'

By this point we should have a fairly good idea about what the problem is, and the advantages of being able to overcome it. We now need to find out exactly what it is that we are thinking, what it is that we believe about ourselves and the problem, and how these beliefs contribute to maintaining it.

5. *Now write down your feelings about the problem.*

'This problem makes me feel Anxious, nervous, tense, afraid, stupid, frightened.'

6. *'What does this mean to me?'*

Lizzie started by writing:

'I will be too nervous and do the paper badly.'

She then asked herself:

'What does this mean to me?'

'People will think I am no good at my job.'

'What does this mean to me?'

'Eileen will think I am no good at my job.'

'What does this mean to me?'

'Eileen will think I am stupid.'

'What does this mean to me?'

'I can't cope with a challenge and show what I can do.'

'What does this mean to me?'

'I will end up losing my job.'

'What does this mean to me?'

'I will have to go back to teaching.'

'What does this mean to me?'

'I am so hopeless that I will fail at that too.'

'What does this mean to me?'

'I will always fail at everything interesting I try.'

'What does this mean to me?'

'I will be unemployed or end up doing some really dull, boring job.'

'What does this mean to me?'

'I am a hopeless failure and it's only a matter of time until everyone finds out.'

'What does this mean to me?'

'I shouldn't waste my time trying to do interesting and fun things. I am basically hopeless and the sooner I realize it, the better.'

This is David's problem and how he discovered his underlying beliefs using the laddering technique.

'I have a new partner. We have been together about a year. Before we met she was married. Her husband and their mutual friends were quite smart and sophisticated. He works in management consulting and is well dressed and stylish. In comparison I feel very scruffy and rough. This makes me off-hand and rude sometimes when I am with them. I know their divorce was amicable but I am afraid that their friends will think I am not good enough for her and that she is only with me on the rebound. We have been invited to a party at one of the old friend's houses. I know I should go but I really don't want to and I am terrified of meeting them all and of what they will think of me. They all have university degrees and fancy jobs.'

The *positive* advantages of solving this problem are:

'If I can overcome my fear of these people then I know that my self-confidence will be increased. I know they are important to Maggie and I would like to have a successful evening with them. I know in my mind that they are not better than me and I would be proud of myself if I could mix with them and feel relaxed and confident. I will be letting myself and my family down if I allow myself to feel inferior. I should feel honoured that Maggie wants to introduce me to them. I don't want to let her down by being difficult and chippy.'

The benefits of not solving the problem are:

'If I don't go to the party then I will not have to face my fears and insecurities. If I go and the evening is a failure, then I can say to Maggie, I told you so, and she won't be able to make me do such a thing again. I will have "inoculated" myself against having to have anything more to do with these people.'

The *costs* of these benefits are:

'It will be damaging for my relationship with Maggie. These are her friends and they are important to her. I will also feel bad about myself and I think that Maggie will think less of me.'

David's first thoughts were:

'People at the party will think I'm dull.'

'What does mean to me?'

'They will think Maggie made a wrong decision by being with me.'

'What does this mean to me?'

'They might be right, I am not good enough for her.'

'What does this mean to me?'

'Maggie will realize that I am not good enough for her.'

'What does this mean to me?'

'She will leave me.'

'What does this mean to me?'

'I will be lonely.'

'What does this mean to me?'

'I will end up alone and unloved.'

In this way Lizzie and David have found out what the underlying beliefs are beneath their anxieties.

Beliefs like these usually remain subconscious and operate automatically. If we want to make them explicit and get them 'out in the open', we actually have to try quite hard. This is because we are generally not aware of them, we usually don't think about them, we don't talk about them, and we don't question them or purposefully try to change them.

Of course, not all of Lizzie's and David's underlying beliefs are negative. Some must be positive or else Lizzie would never have managed to get through college, work as a teacher and then make a change to a job she found more satisfying. David must have some good self-beliefs to have entered into and sustained a relationship with Maggie in the first place. However, the fact that they are both so anxious and lacking in confidence indicates that some fine-tuning of their thoughts may well be extremely helpful for reaching their goals – of self-confidence in David's case and a successful presentation of her paper in Lizzie's case.

If they can change their underlying beliefs and thoughts so that they are working *for* them instead of *against* them, they should both see a very real improvement in confidence. Of course, Lizzie will still have to work hard to write and present a good paper, and David will have to make contact and talk to people at the party, but increased confidence will help them both greatly in these tasks.

This laddering exercise is very powerful, but it can be quite difficult to do. The problem is that as the key beliefs are underlying and subconscious you may not really be in touch with them, and if you don't know what they are, you can't actively change them. A good way to uncover these beliefs is to focus on the feelings we get from a situation. These feelings are often easier to identify than the thoughts themselves. Once you have a good understanding of your feelings, it is usually much easier to identify the thoughts and beliefs. If you have a problem with this exercise, go back to the feelings stage and try to work out exactly how the problem makes you feel.

Disputing negative thoughts and replacing them with PETs

We need to *actively* change any negative beliefs that we have and replace them with positive self-talk (or performance-enhancing thoughts).

Now that David has an understanding of exactly what he thinks and believes about the problem, he can start to change his thoughts and beliefs. The greater our understanding of the problem, the more likely it is that we can devise the correct solution.

David needs to devise an effective counter to his beliefs and thoughts. He needs some positive PETs to destroy his ANTs.

Firstly, he needs to target the more obvious self-talk statements. These are the things that we say to ourselves, such as 'This is too hard, I'll never get this right.' We can change our negative automatic thoughts into performance-enhancing thoughts by consciously saying simple positive things to ourselves *as we work through the problem or the situation.* Examples could include, 'I can do it,' 'Work now, play later,' 'Keep concentrating,' 'Be confident.' David can talk to himself in an encouraging and positive manner. The more he does this, the less room there is for the negative statements to surface. This may feel silly or strange at first, but if he does it over a period of time, it will have powerful effects on how he thinks.

The main thing is to give yourself encouraging self-talk statements that will guide you through the problem situation.

You need short, positive statements about yourself and the problem. If you say these statements over and over to yourself when you are preparing yourself for the problem, or when you are already in the situation, they will counter the negative effects of the ANTs, and eventually replace them. This is a simple but powerful technique for changing your beliefs. It takes some initial effort, but it will pay off in the long run.

It takes some initial effort, but it will pay off in the long run.

What does the research show?

There has been a tremendous amount of research into the effectiveness of techniques for altering self-defeating thought patterns by first identifying negative self-talk statements and then developing adaptive self-talk statements. Based on more that 6,700 research articles since 1963, with both children and adults, we can now say that these techniques are powerful ways to deal with a wide range of problems, including depression,[7] anxiety[8] and test anxiety.[9] What's more, you can use these techniques in organizations[10] and they are useful for enhancing academic performance with schoolchildren and university students.[11]

Short Specific Simple

The key to success in this is to make your PETs simple, specific and short (SSS). This way they will be easy to remember, easy to use, and will have the greatest effect.

Lizzie could dispute her ANT like this:

'I will feel so nervous.'
'Everyone feels nervous, it shows that I am taking the task seriously.'

'People will see I am afraid.'
'Most people are a little bit afraid of public speaking.'

'People will think that I am stupid because I am not a trained botanist.'
'I am not employed as a botanist but as an educator. I am trained as a teacher.'

We also need to deal with the underlying beliefs. We can do this by *disputing* them. If our core underlying belief is (say) *'I'm worthless if I don't do well in the presentation,'* we can challenge this. Ask yourself: 'Is this really true?'

We can also ask things like:
'Are these beliefs helpful?'

In what way are these beliefs inaccurate?

'I will make a mess of this presentation.'
'I am trained as a teacher. I have been good at presenting things to my pupils.'

'I will be so nervous I will fail.'
'I have been nervous before in my teaching. I have managed to cope.'

'My boss will think I'm stupid.'
'She has shown that she has confidence in me by asking me to do it. She wouldn't have done this if she thought I was stupid.'

'My boss will wish she hadn't appointed me.'
'She has told me how pleased she is to have me on board.'

To make this process easier Lizzie could write this out in table format.

Event	ANTs	Feelings	Evaluate ANTs How are they inaccurate? How are they unhelpful?	New PETs
Giving talk at conference	I'm going to mess it up, I'll make a mess of the presentation, and I'll look like a fool in front of everybody and my boss.	Very anxious reluctant to prepare for the talk	The ANTs are not accurate – I'm trained to teach, and I've been good at presentations in the past. The ANTs are not helpful – they make me feel nervous and I procrastinate, which makes it worse.	It's OK to feel a bit anxious – anxiety is just a form of excitement. It doesn't have to perfect – near enough is good enough. I've given good talks in the past – I can do it again

In what way are these beliefs unhelpful?

'I will make a mess of this presentation.'
'Worrying about making a mess makes it more likely to happen.'

'I will be so nervous I will fail.'
'I am allowed to make some mistakes.'

'My boss will wish she hadn't appointed me.'
'She is more experienced than that.'

'She will see how stupid I am.'
'I am not stupid, just nervous.'

Sarah is trained as a window dresser. After working for some years at Harrod's in London she decides to go freelance. She is quite successful and gets several commissions to work on displays and exhibitions. Then through a friend she is asked to work with a stylist on a fashion shoot. The job is in Thailand. She is terribly excited but also very nervous. Although she has worked with fashion before, she feels she is not really trained as a stylist. She wants to do the job because it might lead to more work as a stylist, which is what she would really like to do. But her negative self-talk says:

'I don't have the training.'

'I won't be as glamorous as the other people, the photographers and models.'

'I don't have the confidence and communication skills to do the job properly.'

Through the laddering and disputing techniques she manages to replace these negative thoughts with other, more useful ones. They are:

'I have worked for years with fashion and seen the trends come and go.'

'I know I am good at my job.'

'They want me for my design skills, not my communication skills.'

'I know that modelling is not glamorous, but hard work.'

She manages to hold on to these positive thoughts. She does the job and although it is hard work she loves it and is very successful. The photographer says he would like her to work for him as one of the stylists on his next shoot.

Behavioural effectiveness inventory

You can use this technique to assess how effective your behaviour is. Here's an example. John wanted to get promoted to the next management level in his organization. Although he was more than qualified for the promotion, he felt anxious and uncertain about applying. He knew that other people were interested in the promotion opportunities, and he wanted to get his application perfect to ensure that he did in fact get the job. He found himself caught up in a cycle of anxious thinking and behaviour that was not helpful. He decided to stop and take a behavioural effectiveness inventory – a kind of emotional reality check. This is what he wrote:

Behaviour 'What I did'	Why did I do this?	Consequences of what I did	How effective?	New, improved behaviour
Went around the office gathering advice and feedback from people before acting.	Thought that if I asked enough people I'd be guaranteed not to make the wrong move – asking lots of people is a way to put off actually doing an unpleasant task.	Took considerable time – didn't act on advice anyway.	Spent too much of my own time wasting others' time. People resented my not acting on their advice – I was perceived as being an anxious 'talker' rather than confident 'doer'.	Be highly selective about who I ask for advice – do an emotional reality check before asking for advice.

Identifying these issues helped John focus on acting in a way that moved him towards his goals. He found that acting in a more positive, goal-directed way actually made him feel more confident and less anxious. Managing his behaviour and his emotions, and presenting himself as the kind of person who should get promotion, became a central part of his action programme, and in fact he did get the promotion.

Building a solid House of Change

The environment has a significant impact on how we think, feel and behave. If you drive a car regularly no doubt there have been thousands of times when you've found yourself stopped at the traffic lights but did not make any concious decision to stop the car. It just happened because the traffic lights went to red – the environment gave you the cues as to how to behave – and you followed without even being aware of it.

If you drive the same route to work every day, you probably know how difficult it can be to take another route – say to pick something up from a shop which is a bit out of your way – because you're used to driving one particular route. You have to make a concious effort to change the route you take, and often you forget unless you have something in the car to remind you.

Making a real change – changing the way we think, feel and behave – can be difficult, not because we are stupid, lazy or weak but just because we are busy people who are used to doing things in a certain way in certain situations.

So one way to increase our chances of making changes is to purposefully structure the situation or environment so that it helps us.

STEP SIX

Turn your ANTs into PETs

Task: try out the laddering technique on a problem that is bothering you.

Task: turn your ANTs into PETs

Task: write out three PETs and pin them up somewhere so that you will see them every day.

07

chapter seven
solutions, solutions, solutions

coach yourself

moment.um

Moving away from the problem, towards a solution

Traditionally when faced with a problem we tend to try to analyze and understand it. We try to take it apart and see what has caused it. Coaching uses the solutions-focused approach to dealing with problems. It says:

'Instead of looking at the problem, let's look at the solution.'

By trying to deconstruct a problem, we almost inevitably end up blaming someone or something. This is especially true of problems of human interaction. The trouble with blame is that people feel accused, which makes them defensive and offended. Often because of this we just can't move forward. If instead of apportioning blame we try to look for a workable solution to the problem, we can move on from the difficulties into a better framework.

Solution-focused coaching has been developed from a psychotherapy called brief solution-focused therapy.[1] This approach has been used extensively and with very good result in the fields of education,[2] child behavioural problems,[3] drug counselling,[4] and many other areas. Practitioners found that labelling people as sick often perpetuated the problem.[5]

The solution-focused approach says that when faced with a difficult situation you need to:

◆ clarify your goals

◆ decide what you want to change

◆ see the problem as something you have (not are)

◆ focus on times when you have coped

◆ chart your progress towards the solution

- clarify the central goal or issue
- look at your strengths and successes.

It also means that:

- instead of dwelling on a problem you need to work on finding a solution
- you may need to try several different solutions until you find one that is right for you
- you need to find and use any resources that can help you build solutions
- you need to look at times in the past when you have encountered similar problems and dealt with them successfully
- you need to simplify your problem, break it down into its component parts.

You can apply solution-focused thinking to every area of your life. Sometimes it is so easy it almost feels like cheating.

Julia is a high-powered executive in a business services corporation. She is also the mother of a two year old. She is having trouble getting the child dressed in the morning. He kicks and screams and doesn't want to put on his clothes. She spends some time trying to understand why he doesn't want to get dressed. Perhaps he doesn't want her to go out, he is frightened. It could be any number of reasons, but the child is too young to explain. The mother feels frustrated and as if she has failed. She can't understand why she can handle a department of 30 staff at work but she can't persuade a toddler to get dressed. They are starting every day with a fight. This is distressing for both of them.

Julia has just completed a personal development programme at work. Part of the programme looked at the solution-focused approach to mangement issues. She decides to use the techniques at home.

Using a solution-focused approach Julia looks to see when the child is already getting dressed without a fight. He is more likely to co-operate in getting dressed after his evening bath. So first she goes out and buys three sets of soft cotton trousers and tops. She puts one set on the child each evening after his bath and before he goes to bed. When he wakes up in the morning he is already dressed. The morning fight has vanished.

We need to look at and envisage a solution rather than concentrating on the problem. The irony is of course that it is often by finding the solution that we understand the problem. Think of a crossword puzzle. As soon as you have the answer the clue is obvious. But you might have spent hours trying to work it out. Experienced crossword puzzlers often use the solution-focused approach. They have some inkling of what the answer might be, guess at a word, see if it fits and then see if it explains the clue.

Some scientific research is also done this way.

- A phenomenon is observed, e.g. when an apple falls from a tree it lands on the ground (or your head).
- A theory is constructed that might explain this fact.
- The theory is tested by looking at other phenomena and seeing if they fit into the overall theory.

In other words, we have a clue as to where the answer or solution to the problem might lie. We look in that area and construct an answer. Then we see if it works. If not, change the answer and try something else.

It seems to make sense. But so often we feel we must understand the problem fully before even attempting an answer. We don't realize, or don't allow ourselves to see, that we may be able to solve the problem without ever understanding it, or that it is only by solving the problem that we can understand it.

Traditionally the fire service has been a male-dominated profession. This means that the culture is still very 'masculine'. The one area of the service that has more women workers is the call centre. But political moves, the current climate and equal opportunities legislation means that all the emergency services need to recruit, train and retain more women firefighters, and firefighters from ethnic minorities. Several award-winning advertising campaigns have been launched but have failed to significantly increase the number of recruits from the two target groups.

If this problem were to be magically solved, the fire service would be a dynamic, modern organization, representing and serving all areas of the community.

So some solutions to the problems of recruiting women and ethnic minority groups might be:

◆ a radical revision of the uniform, away from the 'macho', militaristic look

◆ firefighters to wear uniform only in certain circumstances and on certain occasions

◆ the introduction of a 'flatter', less hierarchical management structure

◆ the introduction of lightweight, modern equipment

◆ emphasis on personal development and training

◆ an improvement in communication skills.

In other words, to create a more modern, flexible environment that reflects the world in which the service is operating.

The problem may have been that not enough women or ethnic minorities are represented, but the solution is more than just rectifying this. The solution involves updating and redesigning the whole service.

Sometimes it feels easier and more satisfying to blame someone or something for a problem.

Sometimes it feels easier and more satisfying to blame someone or something for a problem instead of finding a solution. In fact, by apportioning blame we very often absolve ourselves of any responsibility for finding a solution. We have already decided it is impossible.

Imagine this

Your boss leaves and you expect to be promoted. To your surprise and dismay the management appoint someone from outside the company without even considering you for the position (it happens all the time). You feel angry, undervalued and unappreciated. The standard of your work goes down, your motivation vanishes and you feel like leaving.

But it is a good organization, you could do with another year or two there. You like the environment and the culture in which you work.

Apply the solution-focused approach. You are not being valued, so raise your profile. Put some extra effort into your work. When you do something good, make sure people know about it, get yourself sent on some training courses, develop your skills, become an expert at what you do. Read about improving your interpersonal skills and put what you read into practice. Meanwhile start doing research into moving jobs.

Sooner or later people are going to notice you. If they don't, you are in a prime position to switch companies and apply for another job elsewhere. Probably on a higher salary.

Does it work?

A great deal of research has been done into the approach and it has been proved to be an effective approach to change.

What does the research show?

Studies[6] have shown the solution-focused approach to be effective in therapeutic and other applications – figures indicate that clients report improvement in 60–80 per cent of cases. These studies have been carried out in a wide variety of settings, including mental health, school behaviour problems, anger management, family and marital therapy, occupational health and rehabilitation, problem drinking and prison. These figures are as good or better than comparative treatments, and were mostly achieved in between one and five sessions. Interestingly, in all but one of the studies the work was implemenred by relatively inexperienced workers, in many cases just recently trained.

Life coaching is a positive and optimistic approach to dealing with change. It takes the approach that people:

◆ are basically functional, not dysfunctional

◆ have the skills to effect change

◆ can learn to focus on and move towards the kind of life they want to lead

◆ are probably already doing something to move towards the goals they want to achieve.

Miracles happen

The Miracle Question[7] is a powerful, solution-focused technique for developing change. It goes like this.

Suppose that after your normal day's work you go home and go to sleep. When you wake up in the morning a miracle has taken place. Your problem has been solved. Your life is now as you want it to be.

What are the first things you notice that tell you this miracle has happened?

A man in his mid-thirties works for a large multinational computer consultancy. He enjoys his work but often finds it very pressurized. His job is to put together tenders for new contracts. Success for him and his team means that the company wins the contract. His job consists of managing the project, drawing expertise from all sorts of people and putting together a convincing bid. The bid itself is written up in a lengthy document that is then sent to the client. The man has an editorial team with secretarial back-up, but he often finds that he is having to do a lot of the fine detail himself, proofreading the document and so forth. It is vital that the document is accurate and looks professional.

For him the answer to the Miracle Question was:

'I would have an editorial team I could rely on to get the tenders put together properly every time. I wouldn't have to worry about the finer details of getting this done.'

He sees that the long-term solution to his problem is to put in place new systems and procedures that will work across the board.

Some more answers to the Miracle Question.

'I wouldn't have so many different tasks to work on. I would be able to concentrate on one thing without worrying that everything else was just being ignored. Also I'd have more time to go to exhibitions and to stock up on my own creative reserves.' Maggie, creative director, website design company

'I'm not getting cought up in the minor hassles of work so much. I seem to be able to leave work problems at work. I have a new sense of perspective which allows me to remember that work is just work, but family is the really important thing in my life.

Because I'm less of a perfectionist at work I am getting more done, and the quality is pretty much just as good as it always was – no one's said anything derogatory; in fact, several people have commented on how much more relaxed I am.

Because I refuse to work really late anymore, I have more time for my family. Family life is more fun, we're all getting on better, and because there's more harmony at home I come to work feeling refreshed.'

Steve, accountant

Eric is the CEO of a major government organization. He knows that one of his weaknesses as a leader is that he tends not to really listen to what his subordinates say. He anticipates the flow of the conversation, interrupts and jumps to conclusions too quickly. He wants to be a more effective leader. He's tried to force himself to listen and not interrupt, but his attempts never seem to last very long. He's aware of the costs of not improving his leadership skills, and he's keen to get the improvement in team functioning that he knows will come if only he can change. He decides that what he needs is to structure the environment to help him listen more.

Looking to make small but significant changes to the environment, he changes his seating position at the board meeting, and moves from the head of the table to off-centre in the middle. This changes the dynamics of the meeting. He no longer sits in the 'power position'. He also buys a small plastic ear which he has mounted on a block of wood and puts on the table. This causes some amusement, but also shows Eric's subordinates that he is truly committed to change – he is walking the walk rather than just talking the talk.

The Miracle Question will help you to find out what it is you want out of life. Or how things would feel if the problem were solved. It can be used with groups as well as individuals. You could use it on a specific problem or on one area of your life and work.

By looking forward to a solution instead of staying stuck in the problem, we might find not only the answer to what is troubling us but a better outcome than we could ever have imagined.

It is easy to feel that our problems are insoluble.

It is easy to feel that our problems are insoluble, that dreams are all very well but you've still got the mortgage to pay, the kids to look after or whatever. But if you ask yourself,

'If all the obstacles disappeared what would I do?'

then you begin to supply yourself with a solution, even if it is something you will have to work towards. By looking at various solutions, you might just come up with something that will lead you forward. You need to step outside the problem. This is often how discoveries are made and inventions are dreamed up. Someone has the imagination, ingenuity or whatever it is to look at the problem in a way that no one else has thought of.

'We can't solve problems by using the same kind of thinking we used when we created them.'
Albert Einstein, physicist

In his book *Clock This*,[8] Trevor Baylis describes how he first had the idea of a clockwork radio, his simple idea that has revolutionized the lives of millions. He was watching a TV programme about the devastation caused by AIDS in Africa. The narrator described how one of the main problems was getting health education to remote villages. Many villages had no mains electricity and batteries were expensive and could be hard to come by. Solar power wasn't the answer as most people listened to the radio in the evening after dark. Trevor thought about the old wind-up gramophones and how much sound they could produce.

'I had this glaring flash of something so obvious a child of six could have thought of it. If a clockwork gramophone can produce that volume of sound, then why not apply the principle to building a spring-driven radio.

The key to success is to risk thinking unconventional thoughts.'

Trevor Baylis, inventor of the clockwork radio

Life coaching focuses on constructing solutions, not deconstructing problems

This means that:

- the solution is more than merely the absence of the problem
- you need to work towards the solution, rather than moving away from the problem
- chances are you have the abilities necessary to reach your goals, despite the fact that you may not acknowledge these.

The solution-focused approach can be applied to giving presentations.

A lot of people people hate giving presentations. But it is part of the job for many of us. How can you use the solution-focused approach to get over this problem?

Don't try to work out why you hate it, don't compare yourself to others who seem to do it better.

1. Acknowledge that you find it difficult, give the problem some of your time.

2. Prepare as well as you can. Practise on your friends and family.

3. Get colleagues to rate you on a scale from one to ten as to how nervous you seem. You will be surprised. Nerves often don't show as much as you think.

4. Work on finding relaxation techniques that work for you – deep breathing, visualization, etc. Like everything else these get better with practice.

We often feel that to solve a problem we need to fully understand it, to 'get to the root of it'. But sometimes we simply can't understand it. We can go round and round in circles trying to decide what is wrong when what we need is a way out. We need to see the way ahead. By staying stuck in the problem, trying to understand it, we allow ourselves to procrastinate and not deal with issues that are troubling us.

It is a matter of viewpoint.

Problem, what problem?

The first step can be to reassess the situation and look at what we mean by 'problem'. A problem is often simply a way of describing a set of circumstances. The point is that sometimes by looking for creative solutions to the situation in which we find ourselves we can solve problems without ever needing to understand why they came about. The irony is of course that it is often by solving a problem that we start to understand its cause.

What is a problem? Problems are the result of people discussing things in certain ways, ways which build up these things into what they call 'problems', with all that implies. It might be more helpful to think of them and talk about them as stuck patterns – of acting, thinking and speaking.

And so we might talk about the 'problem' as a set of circumstances in which we have yet to find the right way forward. Then there's the suggestion that knowledge of the 'problem' is a necessary and important part of constructing the 'solution'. This is not necessarily the case. Strangely, the more you talk about problems, the bigger and more intractable they can become.

Exceptions

One way of working out solutions to problems is to look at exceptions, times when the problem *didn't* occur. Then work out what you were doing then that made the situation better, and do more of that. So if there were any times when you didn't mind giving a presentation or you even managed to enjoy it, why was that, what did you do differently? Do more of that. If you feel depressed, think back to a time or a day or an hour when you didn't feel so bad. Why was that? What did you do differently? Do more of that.

What did you do differently? Do more of that.

Imagine you have been working late every day. You are fed up and want to go home on time. The first thing to do is to notice if there are any days when you do manage to leave on time. These are your 'special' days. Then try to predict each day whether or not it is going to be 'special'. If a day is special why is it? What is different about these days? Then try to replicate whatever it is about these days on the other days (e.g. no meetings after 4pm). Keep a note of how many times in one month you get home early.

The key is not necessarily to invent strategies but to re-orient yourself. Notice what works well, what you do well. It may be that the improvements are accidental. It doesn't matter – if it works, do more of it. Build on your strengths. Allow other people to use their strengths. Acknowledge that we all have different ways of doing things. If you show respect to the people you work with they will respect you.

It all sounds so simple and it is, but simple doesn't always mean easy.

The first steps are not necessarily the answer. The attitude is, 'Let's do this to find out what happens'. It may lead to the solution. Start small. Take small steps in one direction, then ask yourself, 'Is it working?'

'Anyone who has never made a mistake has never tried anything new.'
Einstein

In the United States, military helicopters flying in a mountainous region kept crashing into the sides of the mountains. The cause was poor communications within the team. Incredibly, everyone could see what was happening but no one pointed it out.

The solution was to build in a formal communications structure that teams were trained in and learned to use automatically. Teams would have to say to one another at strategic points, 'Have you done such and such? and answer yes or no. Some of the things seemed so obvious, but that was precisely why they had been missed. The result was a massive (50 per cent) reduction in crashes.

Mistakes occur everywhere, and this includes hospitals. The wrong medication or the wrong dosage can result in patient death. The solution-focused approach to this problem is used in some hospitals in the USA. Medical staff have formal communications systems to make sure they are using the right medication at the right dosage. Hospitals that use this system report a reduction in errors of up to 90 per cent. In order to develop this system hospitals had to admit their previous errors and instead of apportioning blame and looking for scapegoats, work on a feasible solution to the problem.

STEP SEVEN

Focus on the solution

Task: for each life area you decided to work on ask yourself the Miracle Question:

'If I woke up tomorrow and I had the solution, what would my life look like?'

and then

'How would I know I had the solution?'

'How would other people know that I had the solution?'

chapter eight
gathering strength

Working out where your resources lie

If you are going to make changes in your life you need to draw on your strengths. You need to build your resources. Resources could be personal experience, mentors, influential people in your life, teachers, books, painting, music. Look at your life and work our where your resources lie, where your strength comes from. It is important to know what matters to you. Different things are important to different people. We all get our strength from different places. The key is to trust yourself to know what it is that you need. Look at the things that have got you through so far. Use these resources.

'The main thing that keeps me going is my family. They are what makes it all worth while. But apart from that, walking is important to me. I put my Walkman on, some dance music, something up-beat, and I'm off. Hard work is important too. I am a great believer in just getting on with it, not sitting around moaning.

For a while things were really tough and I worked as a cleaner. From morning to night cleaning other people's houses. It does get quite lonely. You're there cleaning away while they are getting on with their lives. But I used to listen to Radio 4 all day long. It was intelligent, interesting, something to keep my mind going.

Maya Angelou. I find her books an inspiration. She has been through so much and she is a successful woman. A black woman in a white society. And of course my partner. He is always positive, no matter how hard things are. Your health, your happiness, your kids' health. Those are the things that are important.

I always wanted to run a successful business. That was my dream. And to make good money. It's been hard work but I have made it and those were all the things that kept me going.'

Louise, 41, events organizer

Ask yourself, 'What would I miss most if it were to disappear?'

'I have to say the thing that keeps me going is music. I can't say what kind because it depends on my mood. I love Mahler, for his passion, but also sometimes I like the purity of Bach, John Rutter, oh there's loads of them.

I believe in deep relaxation. Self-hypnosis, that sort of thing. I think it helps you to deal with any really stressful problem. to allow yourself to be still and listen to what's going on inside. I have got various relaxation tapes I use.

Of course friends. I've got some really good friends, who I've known for years. One of my friends in particular, he always makes me feel better. No matter what. We've just had some great times together.

I think colour is important, and gardening, flowers bring such joy and brightness into your life.

I'm a great believer in water. The sound of water, drinking lots of water, being beside water. Does that sound odd? But it's so important to me.

Oh yes Shakespeare. I had a great Shakespeare lecturer at college and I still turn to the bard at difficult times.'

Veronica, 36, musician.

Resources are a ray of sunshine

Write down your goal in the centre of a large piece of paper. From this centre draw rays. Along each ray write down a resource, something that will help you move nearer to your goal. You can use this as a kind of mind map.[1]

Resources

Supportive friends
Go to the gym
Laugh more
I am willing to keep trying
I can meditate
Go roller blading
Goal = Less stress
I am learning to delegate more
Take long walks
My family
Listen to music
See the latest movies

Figure 8.1 Map of your resources

'My partner, my kids, going out with my mates. Music, nice clothes. Driving in my car on a sunny day with the music turned up loud. One of my friends died when we were young and I still think of him sometimes. Just the fact that he's not here now and I am. I want people to be happy around me.'

Scott, 27, supervisor at Terminal 4, Heathrow Airport

Some people find that their strength comes from inside.

'When I have a big project on, I don't really look outside myself, I don't look to other people. For me it is very inner. It is a matter of being focused, of being very still and clear inside myself and of having a strong sense of purpose. I want my life to be moving forward. I don't want to let myself down. I become very calm inside. Of course, I do have creative storms along the way, terrible turmoil, but when I actually give the lecture, present the work, I am very calm.

What drives me forward is the beauty and the fascination in the pictures themselves. I just love the feeling of switching these city kids on to art.

It isn't one picture or one painter that inspires me. I get drawn in to whatever I am working on.

Hermione, museum educator, Metropolitan Museum of Modern Art, New York

Some resources are obvious – a partner, a parent, an encouraging friend.

Some resources are obvious – a partner, a parent, an encouraging friend. Others may be more distant but no less important – a teacher who encouraged you at school, a writer you admire, influential people whom you have read about and felt inspired by.

'Keep away from people who try to belittle your ambitions. Small people always do that, but the really great make you feel that you, too, can become great.'
Cicero, *De Senectute*, ch. 7, sct. 24, 44 BC

Perhaps there are specific books that you need or can use to move you closer to your goal. For example, if your goal is fitness, is there a particular sport or fitness plan that you would like to follow? Are there particular sportsmen or women whom you admire? Recipe books you need or want? You might also list particular resources such as libraries, web sites or bookshops that will help you towards your goal.

It may be a way of life, or a style of living that helps you.

'Routine and order are important to me. I like to know how my day is going to be laid up. If I can sort of divide it up into different segments and have something interesting to do in each part of the day, then I am happy.

Family is important to me. That goes without saying, and my friends. And books of course. I like to read a lot. But it is that sense of order and calm that I really love.

I hated it when we had the builders in and everything was all over the place. I really find it hard to cope in that kind of situation.'
Anna, 34, mother

Some people gain their strength in ways that the rest of us cannot even imagine. At 31, Susan was diagnosed with cancer. She recovered and has been well for ten years.

'I would say without a doubt that it was my illness that gave me strength. When I was ill I had to go inside myself and learn how to deal with the fear. No one could help me. I was completely alone and the fear was overwhelming. And I really learned then that nothing is as bad as the fear makes it seem, but that it is the fear itself that is so impossible to deal with. I was literally fighting to survive. I knew I had to get to some still and inner part of myself and if I didn't make it I would die. No one can teach you that, no one can tell you what it feels like. You have to go to that place, the centre of yourself, to find out who you really are. If there is a God then that is what it is, that oneness with the world. That inner stillness. I was lucky, I got better, I survived, and through that experience I gained a strength that no one can take away.'

Susan, 31

It is all so diffuse and hard to get a grip on. It can seem vague and pointless, but all great thinkers and doers have known that the real strength, the real mystery of life, is something quite abstract. Again and again scientific research has demonstrated that concepts that seem mystical and far-fetched actually have a solid basis in fact. Stroke victims are taught to visualize the healing process in order to activate parts of their brains that have been damaged, while meditation has been scientifically proven to reduce stress. It seems very soft, but the effects are hard-edged and real.

What does the research show?

Research[2] has shown that meditation is really effective at reducing stress, anxiety and depression. People who started to meditate on a regular basis also had increased empathy levels.[3]

For most people social networks – friends and family – are important. Again this is something that we know instinctively, but there is also research to back up our intuition. Research shows that people with a good social network are better able to cope with the stress and trauma caused by divorce than those without.

Time and money are resources. Are you using yours in the most useful way? If, for example, you gave up watching television one night a week, what else could you accomplish in that time? What about if you got up half an hour earlier each day? Would that allow you to achieve something valuable? It is easy to argue that we don't have time to do the things we want to do. Sometimes we have to reorganize our lives to fit in the things that matter.

Sometimes we have to reorganize our lives to fit in the things that matter.

'Writing before dawn began as a necessity – I had small children when I first began to write, and I needed to use the time before they said, "Mama", and that was always around five in the morning.' Toni Morrison, Pulitzer Prize-winning novelist, from an interview in *The Paris Review*

Do you have savings that you can use to help you achieve your goals? Or are you wasting money on things that don't really matter to you? Perhaps you need to do a financial audit on yourself. For one week write down everything you spend. Don't try to change anything, just record it. Raise your awareness of what you are doing. Sometimes this in itself is enough to create change.

Already halfway there?

When you decide to make changes in your life, chances are you have already done some of the groundwork. We've usually already started out along the path, although we may not realize it. If you are unhappy in your job you have probably already started looking out for a new one. If you really wanted to be a professional musician but have been advised 'not to give up the day job', you probably at least have a good knowledge of music in your genre. If you feel you are working too many hours a week you have probably considered ways in which you could cut down and thought about alternatives.

If you really have decided to make a change, you are probably already in the ambivalent stage where you are weighing up the pros and cons.

'I was working as a solicitor in the city. I earned lots of money, had a great flat, fantastic car, expensive holidays. I loved the life that money could bring me. But there was always something that felt unfulfilled. I was often bad-tempered. I don't think I can have been easy to live or work with.

But I knew I didn't want to chuck it all in and go backpacking round the world. Nor did I want to retire to a farm in Wales. I wanted some of the buzz and excitement and money of my job, but I needed more down time, more time to myself. Sounds stupid, but I think I was losing sight of who I really was.

Then my flat got broken into and my cameras were stolen. I had three really good ones. They destroyed a lot of my photographs as well. They just trashed everything. I was devastated.

I realized I had been spending more and more of my time thinking about the way I viewed the world, looking at photographs and going to places where I knew I would find a good picture. It had just crept up on me. It wasn't until some of my best photos were destroyed that I realized how much they meant to me.

I should give those burglars a reward I suppose. Because in some way they really did change my life. I stopped hungering after promotion at work and instead put more of myself into the photography. I "allowed" myself to buy two really good cameras and I acknowledged my interest. I gave it space in my life. Maybe I was ready to do it anyway but the burglary gave me an extra push.

I've even started entering competitions. I haven't won anything yet and maybe I won't. I don't expect to earn my living at it (although you never know), but I have made room in my life for my passion.'

Ian, solicitor

Look at your life, at the goals you have set yourself. Have you already made some progress towards them? You can start to prepare for changes in your life long before you actually make the leap.

'I sent off for prospectuses from different universities, so by the time I left my job I knew the entry qualifications I needed for the various courses I was interested in. I also found out about grants, loans and all that sort of thing.'

Sean, 28, student

Give your project a name

Once you have decided which area of your life you want to work on and have set yourself some SMART goals, you can give your project a name. Naming things makes them real. Different cultures and languages have different names and words for different things. This reflects different views of the world and of reality – the famous 30 different words for snow or whatever. If snow, and different kinds of snow, are important in your life, you need ways of describing their various forms and properties. If you give your project a name you turn it into a real concept, a distinct, identifiable part of your life.

If you give your project a name you turn it into a real concept.

Choose a talisman

Choose an object you can carry around with you that will represent your project. It could be a photograph, a key ring, any small object that will help you remind yourself of your purpose and aims.

What does the research show?

Information in our minds iis organized into clusters of related information[4] called schemas. Say the word 'dog' to someone and they may well think of the word 'cat'. Whatever their response, there's a good chance that at the word 'dog' it will be very much the same.

Our schemas can be unconciously and consciously[5] triggered by signs and symbols, and we can use this to prompt us to continue to make the changes we have planned.

The effects of deliberately placing symbols where we can see them can be powerful. External symbols act as a kind of external memory bank. Studies[6] have shown that using external symbols increased adults' and children's memory recall and when these signs were unexpectedly removed from their memory

▶

performance dropped. Marketing companies[7] have found that if they use visual signs in addition to brand names, children remember the brand for longer – very useful if you want to sell more of your product to kids.

So, using signs and symbols really works.

Give something back

It is important to be able to give back something to the people who have helped you or are helping you to reach your goals. If you acknowledge their help, they will probably be glad they gave it. But as with lots of things, it is often easier not to acknowledge help and support. People may feel it is embarrassing or sentimental just to say to someone, 'Thanks for your help. It meant a lot to me.'

Research shows that what is called 'emotional intelligence' – using your emotions in a constructive and mature way – is a greater indicator of job and life success than any other measure including IQ and educational background. It is a sign of emotional intelligence and maturity to be able to give sincere compliments and acknowledge the support you receive from people around you.

What does the research show?

Recovering alcoholics who have been sober for a few years often 'sponsor' or mentor newly sober individuals. It has been shown[8] that people who sponsor others are more likely to stay sober and report a better quality of life than recovering alcoholics who do not give anything back.

STEP EIGHT

Gather your resources

Task: give each project you are working on a name and a symbol.

Task: look back at situations in the past and list the strengths that have helped you cope.

Task: list your:

◆ physical resources

◆ mental/intellectual resources

◆ emotional resources

◆ spiritual resources

◆ financial resources

◆ situational resources.

chapter nine
staying on track

'A journey of a thousand miles begins with the first step.'

Lao-Tzu, chinese philosopher, c. 550 BC

Take small steps

A common mistake in trying to make life changes is to try to do too much too fast. Try to change too much and your performance will get worse, not better.[1] You need to plan small steps towards your goals. These are less daunting and much more achievable than grandiose plans. Ask yourself, what would be the first small step towards my goal? What about the one after that? And the next one?

Sometimes these small steps may feel almost insignificant but they build up to create something new. This is what life is like, it is lived in tiny steps. At what point does a young person become old? When does a stream become a river? Where exactly is the foot of a mountain? Where does the mountain start? With many if not most things in life there is no single point at which things change. And when there is one pivotal event that tips the balance it is usually caused by a tiny adjustment. It may be the last straw that breaks the camel's back but only because of all the other straws that went before it. Most of life is lived by degrees, by tiny changes. Perhaps this is why ceremony is so important in our lives – we need to create an exact point at which we can say things have changed.

Life is made up of tiny events. It is only in hindsight that we can see which were the significant moments in our lives and how they built up to make a whole story.

'The details are excruciatingly boring I know, but if you want to follow the sinuous route of a single life, if you want to see

where it came from and where it went, it's impossible to tell
what's superfluous and what's indispensable.'   Luis Buñuel, film director[2]

Monitor your progress

Just as we seem to need ceremonies and events to monitor our
progress through life, you need some sort of mechanism to monitor
your progress towards the goals you have set yourself. Apart from
anything else your goals may change or you may find that the things
you are doing to reach them are not working and you need to be able
to adjust them as you go.

Think of long-distance runners. As their stamina improves the
challenges they need to set themselves change. Perhaps they are
getting tired of a particular route or they suffer an injury, which will
mean they need to change their training schedule. The same is true
for any changes you want to make in your life. Once you have
established a vision, examined your values and determined your
goals, you need to set in place a system of assessment and
evaluation. If you don't do this you may quickly find yourself
demotivated if your goals turn out to be unrealistic or inappropriate.
As you reach your goals you need to set yourself new ones.

As you reach your goals you need to set yourself new ones.

'The most important thing to do is set goals. Training is a waste
of time if you don't have goals.'

Samantha Riley, world champion breaststroke swimmer

Scaling

One way of working out how close you are to where you want to be
is to use the scaling technique. You rate how near you are to your
goal on a scale from 0 to 10. At 10 you have reached the goal, at 0 you
are as far away as possible.

Tom has always dreamed of being a writer. He works as a careers adviser at a large college but feels increasingly unfulfilled. He has had various attempts at writing and has sent off some stories to competitions. He has joined a writers' circle which he goes to one evening a week. It sometimes makes him feel further away than ever from his goal as everyone on the course has been writing and talking about writing for years, but no one has ever had anything published.

He rates how near he is to his goal on a scale of 0 to 10. At 10 he would be a successful published writer, living on his earnings from writing. At 0 he would be as far away as he could imagine from this goal. He puts himself at a 3. He has actually completed some work and he once had an article published in a trade journal.

By rating himself as a 3 rather than a 1 or a 2 Tom realizes that he has already made some progress towards his goal. Now he needs to imagine what the next step up the scale might look like.

Although the overall goal might seem large and unattainable, the steps towards it can be quite small. This kind of scaling also allows you to give yourself benefit for movement towards your goal, even if you haven't reached it yet. If you have dreams and aspirations, the chances are you have already moved some way towards achieving them.

Tom decides to sign up for a proper journalism evening class and to do another article for the trade magazine. He also looks at the books available on his subject. He decides to contact some of the publishers and try to get a commission for a book on how students might fill their gap year. It is not the kind of writing he ultimately wants to do but he is moving towards his target.

Next time he rates himself he gives himself a 5.

During the course of your life-coaching sessions you can rate yourself on your progress towards your goal at regular intervals. It is a mechanism that allows you to chart your progress.

GROW

Another technique you can use is the GROW model.[3] You can set aside some time each week to look at your Goals, Reality, Options and Wrap-up.

Figure 9.1 The GROW model

Journals and diaries

A useful way of staying on track is to keep a record in the form of a journal or diary. This does not have to be hugely detailed – short notes written on a daily basis are all you really need, although some people find 'writing it out' in detail helps them to keep moving forward. This kind of progress monitoring has been used for years in clinical psychology.

What does the research show?

Self-monitoring can be a powerful technique for change in almost any area of life.

Self-monitoring has a beneficial effect on mental health. People with problem health behaviours such as smoking, or who feel depressed or anxious, improve if they use self-monitoring.[4] In one study,[5] unskilled novice golfers were asked to monitor their positive thoughts about their golf swings. Their performance improved substantially compared with that of other novice golfers. Law students who were taught to use self-monitoring suffered less stress and displayed better academic performance.[6]

Keeping a journal and monitoring your progress is important, but we also need a way to structure our self-coaching sessions. Structuring the way we work on our self-coaching programme will help us to keep moving forward. We need to take time on a regular basis to examine our progress, set new goals for the week and develop an action plan. We need to take time to grow towards our goals.

Goals

As we saw in Chapter 5 you need to make sure you have set yourself goals that are SMART – specific, measurable, attractive, realistic and time-framed. These goals should be written down. You need to make sure that they are clear and motivating. If they are not then your chances of success are greatly reduced. In the GROW session you take time to look at how you are progressing towards your goals. You can work out the techniques and strategies that are helping you to move forward and get rid of the ones that do not seem to be working for you.

In the part of your GROW session that deals with goals you can ask yourself:

◆ What do I want to achieve in this session?

◆ How do I want to feel afterwards?

◆ What is the most productive way I can spend my time during this session?

◆ What do I want to look at?

Reality

You have your written goals and you are working towards them. You need to look at where you are right now. Do you need to adjust your goals or set new ones? Ask yourself these questions:

◆ What has happened during the past week?

◆ Have I encountered any problems in trying to achieve my targets?

◆ How did I handle the problems?

◆ On a scale of 1 to 10 how well did I handle the problem?

- What is happening in my life at the moment?

- When does this happen?

- What effect does it have on my goals?

- How have I tried to deal with it?

- What worked?

Options

Next you need to look at the available options. You may need to brainstorm this bit to make sure that you look beyond the obvious. Here you need to use solution-focused thinking (*see* Chapter 7).

Ask yourself:

- What is the full range of possible actions in this circumstance?

- Which is the most attractive to me now?

- What are the costs and benefits of taking this action?

If you are experiencing a problem with your goals:

- Are there times when the problem doesn't occur?

- What is different about these times?

- How can I do more of what works for me?

- How have I stopped the problem from completely overwhelming me?

- What has worked for me in the past?

- What can I do to change the situation?

- How can I move towards my goal?

- Who can support me in making this change?

- What are the costs and benefits of this course of action?

Wrap-up

Before you end the session you need to plan what you are going to do next. So:

- List some specific tasks.

- List some people who can support you.

- How will you know if you are being successful?

- What sort of things might stop you being successful?

- What will you do if you find these things are getting in the way?

Ambivalence is a normal and expected part of the change process.

As we said earlier, ambivalence is a normal and expected part of the change process. It is this very ambivalence that can make it hard to make changes. Uncertainty is uncomfortable, but in order to make a change you need to be able to live with uncertainty. There will always be reasons for staying where we are, for staying in the comfort zone, but we have to be prepared to go through some discomfort if we are to change negative behaviour patterns.

'I knew I wanted to do the course, to get educated, to be able to say to people, "Look, I'm not stupid, I can get an education too." But at the same time I was terrified. I suppose there were so many times before when I'd started to do things, make changes, go on courses, but I always gave up. I don't know why but I always found some excuse.

This time I really want to do it but I am afraid. I find myself going down to the JobCentre and looking in the window. I know it sounds stupid, but I have to really stop myself from going in and applying for a job in a shop or something. It is so tempting just to go in and sign up for something, then I'd start earning money again, and go on as I was before.

The difference is that this time there is something that stops me. I know that unless I have some skills and qualifications behind me I am going to be as dispensable as ever. I want to get an education. Something that will stay with me for ever.'

Dinah, 29, retail manager

Here is the GROW session Dinah carried out halfway through her course.

Goals

What do I want to achieve in this session?
Take stock of where I am. Look at areas where I am successful. Work out how I can spend more time on studying.

How do I want to feel afterwards?
Less stressed, with a clear plan. Hopeful.

What is the most productive way I can spend my time during this session?
Look at what work I have left to do.

What do I want to look at?
Time management.

Overall goal?
To successfully complete my degree.

Smart goal for this week
To complete my assignment on time, without staying up all night to get it done.

Reality

What has happened during the past week?
I have completed one assignment.

Have I encountered any problems in trying to achieve my targets?
I found it very difficult and stressful trying to fit the work in.

On a scale of 1 to 10 how well did I handle the problem?

What is happening in my life at the moment?
I have a slight feeling of panic. Perhaps I won't be able to cope.

When does this happen?
When I try to fit in too much.

What effect does it have on my goals?
I end up doing silly things like watching boring programmes on TV to take my mind off things.

How have I tried to deal with it?
Tried to set myself small tasks each day. Like reading a chapter of a textbook.

What worked?
Not trying to achieve too much at once.

Options

What is the full range of possible actions in this circumstance?
I could give up work, take a loan and study full-time.
I could look for part-time work.
I could cut down on my social life. Stay in and work more.

Which is the most attractive to me now?
Cutting down on my social life.

What are the costs and benefits of taking this action?
Costs are I might feel lonely and isolated.
Benefits are I will feel more stressed.

If you are experiencing a problem with your goals

Are there times when the problem doesn't occur?
When I am really interested in the assignment topic I find it easier to study.

What is different about these times?
I feel more confident and motivated.

How can I do more of what works for me?
In future try to carefully choose the courses that match my interests.

How have I stopped the problem from completely overwhelming me?
Talking to other people about it.

What has worked for me in the past?
Sharing my worries with my friends.

What can I do to change the situation?
See if I can find someone on my course who will meet regularly to discuss problems.

Who can support me in making this change?
My boyfriend.

What are the costs and benefits of this course of action?
Costs – I will be spending more time 'socializing', but with a good aim in view. It might feel like I'm wasting my time.

Benefits – I won't feel so isolated. It will help me get my degree.

Wrap-up

List some specific tasks.
Make a study plan for the next month.
Contact some people on my course, see if they want to form a support group.

List some people who can support you.
[Names}

How will you know if you are being successful?
I will feel less stressed and sleep better.

What sort of things might stop you being successful?
If it gets very busy at work I find it hard to come home and study.

What will you do if you find these things are getting in the way?
Try to schedule in the most interesting tasks for the time when work is very busy.
Try to tell myself that a little bit of study every day is better than one great big session once a week.

At the next GROW session Dinah will have to see whether or not the steps she has taken to ease her stress have worked.

Anticipate problems

If you can imagine in advance the sort of problems you might encounter, you are in a much better position to deal with them. It is just a matter of being prepared.

Of course, you can't be prepared for any eventuality. Life has a habit of taking us by surprise. But if you take some time to look at past situations that you have coped with and to analyze the strengths that you used to help you, you will feel more confident in dealing with tricky situations in the future.

You may not necessarily have been successful in achieving your aims, but you may still have used strengths and skills to help you to deal with your situation.

STEP NINE

Staying on track

Task: for each life area plan a series of small steps leading towards your goal.

Task: schedule yourself some appointments (once a week). Use the GROW technique to monitor your progress.

Task: try to work out the obstacles that might get in your way and things that could slow you down. Is there anything you can do about them?

chapter ten
do it with a friend
co-coaching

'Dr Ransome's sandy head ducked as the truck lumbered through the tunnel. Jim was tempted to run after it, but he knew he had decided to stay with Mr Maxted. He had learned that having someone to care for was the same thing as being cared for by someone else.'

J.G. Ballard[1]

What is co-coaching?

Co-coaching is a formalized agreement between two or more people to support, motivate and facilitate change. All the techniques outlined in this book are designed for you to use working on your own. If you stick to the process and work through the programme at the back of the book you will get the results you want. (If you take shortcuts you will significantly reduce the chances of making successful change in your life.) But for some people, and for some goals, it can be useful to work with somebody else. Co-coaching is not necessary or even suitable for everyone. It just might be easier and more fun with someone else.

'I started out on a coaching programme. I went on a course at the university and learned all about setting SMART goals, evaluating my progress, identifying my values, developing a vision, all that stuff. I decided to work on setting up my own gardening business. It is something I have always wanted to do. I've been talking about it for years but I never seemed to get much further than that.

The programme did work. I bought a van and started taking on some clients. But I have to admit it was hard. I have a full-time "day job" as well and I did find it really hard to keep myself motivated. I went back to my tutor on the course and he advised me to try co-coaching. He put me in touch with another member of our group who was trying to set up a similar business.

We agreed to meet once a week for a month. We each drew up a plan outlining what we hoped to achieve. I am finding it is working very well. Having Steve to talk to helps me to see where I want to go and where I might go wrong. I am hoping Steve will agree to renewing our co-coaching contract for another month.'

Robin, teacher/gardener

Why co-coach?

Working with another person can have many benefits, for example:

◆ It can be more motivating.

◆ It gives each person an outside viewpoint.

◆ You may form lasting relationships.

◆ You can share ideas.

◆ It can be more fun.

What does the research show?

A survey[2] of 244 manufacturing managers found that co-coaching and mentoring was positively related to both salary and promotion rate. When teachers use co-coaching on themselves, their teaching skills increase,[3] and when students co-coach each other, their academic performance tends to increase.[4]

It can be quite hard to be objective about your own situation. Co-coaching can help you to see the issues you are dealing with more clearly.

Should I co-coach?

As humans we are all different. You need to adopt the coaching style that is best for you, the one that will help you reach your goals. You probably already know whether or not you are the kind of person who likes to work with somebody else. If you have tried coaching yourself and find that you get stuck or lose motivation, co-coaching can be a useful option.

Who do I co-coach with?

Once you have decided that you do want to co-coach, you need to find a suitable partner or partners. There are no real rules about who you should co-coach with. Anyone with whom you can come to a written agreement about the boundaries of the coaching relationship could be suitable. You could co-coach with a friend, a colleague, a work mate.

You could co-coach with a friend, a colleague, a work mate.

The only real proviso is that coaching must not impact negatively on your relationship. This could mean that you should not coach your partner. And in some circumstances not your work mates, although coaching in the workplace can be much more successful than social relationships because these kinds of relationships are more formalized. It is important to remember that coaching does not equal nagging. Used properly, coaching can dramatically improve communication.

You could decide to co-coach over the telephone or online.

How do I co-coach?

You must have clearly written and defined boundaries about:

◆ how long you are going to co-coach for

◆ how often you are going to meet or speak

◆ what you are going to talk about

♦ how you are going to structure the coaching sessions.

In order to co-coach you must:

♦ draw up a fixed-term agreement of between one and three months

♦ re-commit every month – this is a very important motivator

♦ give permission to the other person to ask you searching and sometimes personal questions about your beliefs and motivation. (But coaching is not therapy. It is not about what happened in your childhood, etc. If this happens then you are going off track.)

Before you start you need to:

♦ draw up a contract for change (*see* Chapter 12)

♦ agree on what you will and won't talk about.

Useful questions to ask are:

♦ 'How could you have done this better?'

♦ 'What's stopping you?'

♦ 'If all the obstacles disappeared, what would you do?'

♦ 'What are your beliefs around this issue?'

♦ 'In what way are these beliefs helpful or unhelpful?'

♦ 'How can you work on changing the beliefs that are unhelpful?'

There must be a safety mechanism so that you can say, 'I don't want to go into that.'

If you co-coach face to face there must be an equal amount of time devoted to each person's issues. The coach has to give 100 per cent attention.

Listening is the key

Listening is the key skill in coaching. The coach has to listen most of the time. This is not as easy as it sounds. You need to get beyond the everyday type of listening, what we call 'level one' listening.[5] Level one listening is where your attention is primarily on yourself – what you want to say, how you feel. But this is not the kind of listening we need to be effective co-coaches. For this we need to be able to put our ego to one side and focus on helping the other person express their thoughts, feelings and plans. This is a much deeper form of listening – 'level two' listening – and like all skills it needs some practice.

If you decide to co-cach you could practise some of the following exercises to help develop your listening skills.

Level one listening

Ask your co-coach to talk about a change in their lives. As you listen, interrupt the person, give them advice, tell them where they went wrong. Listen to your own reactions, your own self-talk, as you are listening to your coaching partner.

Level two listening

Then ask them to tell you about some other aspect of their lives, but talk about the same change. This time listen carefully to the emotional content, and reflect back to them what they are saying. Use the questions above to explore the issues more deeply. Listen carefully to the tone of voice, really tune in to what they are saying. Try to picture what they are talking about.

When you have finished the exercise, swap over. You do the talking, get your partner to do the listening. The benefits of developing good listening skills include:

◆ improved relationships with other people

◆ reduced stress

◆ increased productivity

◆ increased awareness of your own and other people's emotions

◆ richer experience of life.

Use the GROW model

You can use the GROW model (*see* Chapter 9) in your co-coaching sessions. Work out what you really want. Make plans for what to do between sessions.

STEP TEN

Getting help

Task: find someone to co-coach with if you think it is a style of coaching that will suit you.

11

chapter eleven
taking credit for success

Taking the credit for success

Nothing succeeds like success. It is an old adage and it is true of course. The more we succeed in meeting our goals, the more likely we are to believe in ourselves and to meet our goals in the future. But we have to allow ourselves to take the credit for our success and to acknowledge the skills, talent and work that have gone into our achievements. By setting clear, measurable goals, we can see what we have achieved and we can see what it is that has helped us on our way. We can begin to allow ourselves to take credit for what we have done.

What does the research show?

Since 1976 there have been more than 6,100 published research studies looking at the effect of people's confidence on their ability to reach their goals. Self-confidence has been found to be one of the most important factors (and often the single most important factor) contributing to success in almost every area of life, including leadership[1] musical performance,[2] relationships[3] and sports.[4] One study even found that self-confidence predicted performance in snake handling.[5]

So if we want to reach our goals we need to consciously work on developing our sense of competence. One way we can do this is to learn to take the credit for success and not to give ourselves a hard time for setbacks.

Sports psychologists have found that when people win they tend to take the credit for it, saying things like:

'I tried hard.'
'I gave it everything.'
'The training paid off.'

When they lose they are more likely to blame their lack of effort on factors beyond their control, saying things like:

'The referee was biased.'
'It was just bad luck.'

This means that losers are protecting themselves from feeling bad when they lose by blaming events outside their control. Of course, they are happy to take the credit and feel good about themselves when things go well.

Not everyone explains success and failure the same way.

But not everyone explains success and failure the same way. Some people tend to think that any successes they have are just a matter of luck, and any failures are due to personal flaws or inadequacy. Optimistic people who suffer setbacks tend to attribute them to external causes that are temporary and can be changed. On the other hand, when faced with failure, pessimists tend to have hopeless thoughts. They tell themselves, 'I'll never get it right' or 'I always mess it up' or worse, they stamp themselves with a negative label – 'I'm an idiot.'

If you believe that the positive things that have happened to you are simply good luck then you must also feel that if the wind changes and bad luck is blown your way instead, things may start to fall apart. If on the other hand you allow yourself to see what it is you have done to get you where you are then you can start to believe in your own ability to bring about change.

The way we explain our successes and failures is important. It can affect our work performance, relationships, mental health and even how long we live.

What does the research show?

Martin Seligman[6] has spent more than 30 years researching the impact of optimistic and pessimistic explanatory styles. He has found that an optimistic explanatory style – taking the credit for success and not seeing yourself as a failure if you don't reach a goal – has been predictive of excellence in everything from sports to life-insurance sales (a finding that saved Metropolitan Life millions of dollars in personal selection). Also, optimists are more resistant to infectious illness and are better at fending off chronic diseases of middle age. One study looked at 96 men who had their first heart attack in 1980. Within eight years, 15 of the 16 most pessimistic men had died of a second heart attack, but only five of the 16 most optimistic men had died.

The ability to rethink the way we explain events in our lives and the way we choose to focus on failure or success has a very real impact on who we are and how we live our lives.

'I didn't have an easy life as a child. My father was an alcoholic. He frequently became violent and I learned to read the signs and keep out of his way when a black mood was coming over him. My brother's reaction was to go to his room. He just retreated, locked the door and refused to come out. The sad thing is that although he is now an adult, in some ways he is still locked in that room. He is very cut off from the world, he doesn't allow anyone to get close. He lives alone, has few friends and a job he is not stimulated by.

I felt very badly about my childhood for a long time. But then I started to think about what I had actually achieved. I have a good job, a happy marriage, two happy, well-balanced children. I started to realize that I am a survivor. I gave up feeling sorry for myself and started to celebrate my successes instead.

Of course, the hurt is still there. It will never go away, I have memories of terrible times that I would not wish on anyone. But at the same time I can see how strong I have been, how I have come through it all. By writing down all the strengths and skills that I have used to cope with my difficult childhood, I started to feel better about myself.'

Mia, 37

Celebrating success

If we learn to set realistic SMART goals we should have a lot of occasions to celebrate success and it is important that we do so. When we succeed in something we need to allow ourselves to take the credit for our hard work, skills and talent.

Fear of success

Success is not always comfortable and many people are afraid of the discomfort that success might bring. We might feel that we don't deserve to be successful, that other people will envy and dislike us, that the more we succeed the harder we have to push ourselves, that we will lose the purpose, the goal we were striving for, that success will bring difficult and frightening changes that we may not be able to cope with.

Looking beyond the specific goal to our underlying motivation may give us some tools to deal with any fear of success. If we understand that the goals we set ourselves are not our real motivation it may help us to deal with success. This sounds odd at first but look at mountain climbers. Their goal is to reach the top of the mountain. This doesn't mean that when they reach the top they are going to necessarily feel anything except exhaustion. They may in fact feel quite deflated and empty inside. The paradox is that although we need a goal to keep us going, it is not in reaching the goal that the real satisfaction or happiness lies but rather in the movement towards it – the focus, commitment and purpose that having a goal provides. So in a very real sense athletes and sports people do not play to win, they win so that they can play.

Sports psychologists have discovered that if a sports person focuses exclusively on winning, they are almost certain to lose. In a TV interview, tennis champion Martina Navratilova was asked what she thought about when she was playing an important match. She replied that if she turned her thoughts away from the precise moment in hand, the location of the ball, the serve or whatever, in that second the game would be lost. In other words she could not afford to think about winning the match, the set or even the game. She could think only about the precise moment she was in, returning the ball in the best possible way.

If we understand that setting goals helps us create focus and purpose in our lives, it follows that reaching those goals could be uncomfortable, because then the focus, the purpose, has gone.

Welcoming success

Whatever the reason for fearing success it is important to be able to acknowledge and welcome success. How can you do this?

Ted was a successful advertising executive. He won many big accounts for his company and was doing very well. He turned to life coaching partly because he was having trouble managing his time effectively but also because he felt the need to push himself harder and harder to reach his goals but never allowed himself to acknowledge his success. Working on the principle that phobics – people with irrational and exaggerated fears – go to great lengths to avoid the thing they are frightened of, Ted's coach decided to help Ted face the success that he seemed to be so afraid of. He got Ted to look at himself in the mirror once a day and acknowledge his success; for example, say to himself, 'I dealt really well with that tricky client.' He had to do this for a couple of minutes each day and write down how he felt before and afterwards. Gradually Ted found that he could accept and enjoy his success. This in turn allowed him to let up the pressure on himself a little, which in turn helped him to manage his work more effectively as he no longer felt he had to achieve more and more in less and less time. It allowed him to enjoy his success and feel good about himself.

Even if you don't always reach your goals or achieve the things you want to achieve, you can still learn to value the skills and strengths you bring to life challenges. Perhaps you have done the best in the circumstances, even if the outcome is not exactly what you would have wished. Research[7] increasingly shows that wealth, power and fame do not make people happy. It is learning to enjoy what you do that brings real fulfilment.[8]

It is learning to enjoy what you do that brings real fulfilment.

'Success is getting what you want, happiness is wanting what you get.'
Ingrid Bergman, actress

If you set yourself clear goals and live your life according to your own beliefs and values, you will know when you are successful, even if your success is not what other people would have aimed for or wanted.

'I don't see myself as any great example of success. I had just retired and I heard about the courses at the university and I thought, "Why not?" It's there. These opportunities weren't there when we were younger. I left school at 17 and went straight into the civil service. University was for the sons and daughters of doctors and lawyers, not for us.

It wasn't something I had always dreamed of doing or anything like that. I'd done a few night classes and they hadn't been that interesting and I thought this might be something more. It was just a spur of the moment thing. In fact I got my application in on the very last day. The forms and the photograph and everything.

As I say, I don't feel that it is such a great achievement. It was hard going at times, the writing, but they gave us help with that, structure and that sort of thing. Sometimes the writing came easy and flowed, other times it was like chipping away at granite. So yes, it was hard work. But I never had any second thoughts, never had any doubts. Once I started, I was going to see it through.

There was one essay I am proud of. I got 95 per cent on it. I couldn't believe it. Some of the lecturers said to me, "You can't get 95 per cent, it doesn't exist, 90 per cent is the highest we give." But this one professor said, "I wanted to give it 100 per cent, 95 is a compromise, I'm not changing it." I was pleased with that.

Some people said to me, "Good on you" but some thought I was mad. What're you doing that for? Putting yourself through that for? But I would say to anyone, it's there, if you want to do it, do it. Find something you're interested in, film studies, radio, whatever. What have you got to lose?

Thomas, 67, retired civil servant, university graduate

Tracking your successes

You might find it useful to keep a note of your successes and the feelings associated with them. Focusing on positive outcomes is a powerful means of moving forward. It is a way of drawing a line under your actions and moving on to the next goal. If you never allow yourself to stop and take stock of what you have achieved, you deny yourself the satisfaction of reaching your goals.

STEP FOUR

Celebrate your success

Task: find ways to celebrate success on a daily basis and at the end of your project.

12

chapter twelve
coach yourself: a life-coaching programme for change

About the programme

This programme has been tried, tested and developed over five years. Hundreds of people have used this programme (or earlier versions of it) to make significant changes in their lives, and in doing so have given feedback as to what was useful or not useful for them. This feedback allowed psychologists at the University of Sydney, Australia, to fine-tune and further develop the programme, and to discard any techniques and strategies that were too complex or confusing to use. After this extensive development process was complete, the programme as a whole was validated in a scientific study run by the Coaching Psychology unit at the University of Sydney.

What does the research show? Does it really work?

To determine whether the Coach Yourself programme was truly effective, 20 individuals used it to help them make a number of changes in their lives. These changes included starting a new business, enhancing time-management skills, career development, and improving interpersonal skills. On average these people had been trying unsuccessfully to make these changes for 23.5 months. Rating their progress towards goal attainment before and after the programme on a scale from 1 to 5 (5 being total goal attainment), there was a statistically significant difference before and after the Coach Yourself programme. That is to say that completing the Coach Yourself programme really helped these people reach their goals. What's more, there was a statistically significant decrease in depression and stress, even though depression and stress were not specifically targeted in the change programmes.

As well as testing the programme as a whole, all of the individual techniques and strategies in this programme have been empirically validated – that is, they have been shown in scientific studies to be genuinely effective means of inducing change.

This programme is no 'magic bullet', there's nothing mystical, mysterious or complex about it. In fact, it's taken years to make it simple (*see* Figure 12.1).

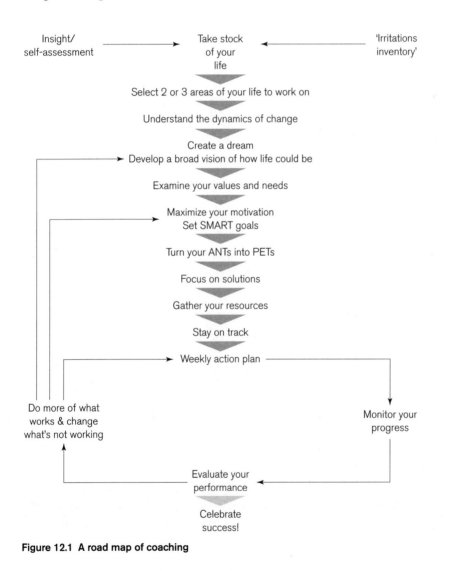

Figure 12.1 A road map of coaching

Keeping it simple

A common mistake in life coaching is to try to change too much, too fast and too soon. Research shows that it is best to make small but significant changes in two or three key areas of your life, and that these small changes inevitably lead to big changes over time. Trying to change your whole life at once will not normally be effective. Small steps lead to big changes. Making two or three small but significant changes in your life spreads the benefits of change throughout your life. It's like dropping a stone into the centre of a still pond – the ripples reach to the very edge.

This programme is based on the following principles:

◆ Make the implicit explicit – examine and question the assumptions we make about our lives and ourselves.

◆ Keep it simple.

◆ Do the least work to make the greatest change.

◆ Focus on solutions not problems.

◆ Don't try to solve the unsolvable.

◆ People are functional not dysfunctional.

◆ People have the abilities to reach their goals, despite the fact that they may not acknowledge these in themselves.

Why you need to 'write it out'

To complete the programme you need to do a fair amount of writing about your thoughts, feelings, dreams and plans. Sometimes people doing this programme feel that actually putting pen to paper is not necessary and that they can make changes and coach themselves without completing the written exercises. It has been my experience that people who do not complete the written exercises are not as successful in making changes – the written exercises significantly contribute to your chances of success. If you skimp on the written exercises you are cheating yourself.

What does the research show?

Written exercises can be a powerful way of creating change. Depressed patients who complete written homework exercises have been found to improve three times as much as those who do not.[1] Writing it out helps make change in a wide range of areas, including panic attacks,[2] test anxiety,[3] and shyness.[4] Of course, it could be that people who complete the written exercises are more motivated to make changes and that is why they get better. But by using sophisticated statistical techniques it has been shown that while individuals' levels of motivation were important, it was the written homework, not the motivation, that caused people to make changes.[5]

Laying the foundations for change

What do we need to create purposeful change? Essentially there are four factors.

1. We need a sense of *discontent with the present*.

    If we are really happy with what we have then why bother changing?

2. We need a broad, inspirational *vision of the future*.

    If we're uninspired by our vision of the future, we're unlikely to put the effort in to create change – if the vision we have is too rigid and specific, it will not allow us the necessary flexibility in the enactment of our action plans.

3. We need the *skills to reach our goal*.

    Here 'skills' means both *skills* and *knowledge*. Without both of these we will have the desire and vision to change, but will not know how to do it.

4. Underpinning both of these is *continuous and deliberate action* towards our goals.

    Creating purposeful, directed change requires *continuous and deliberate action* – not just wishful thinking (*see* Figure 12.2).

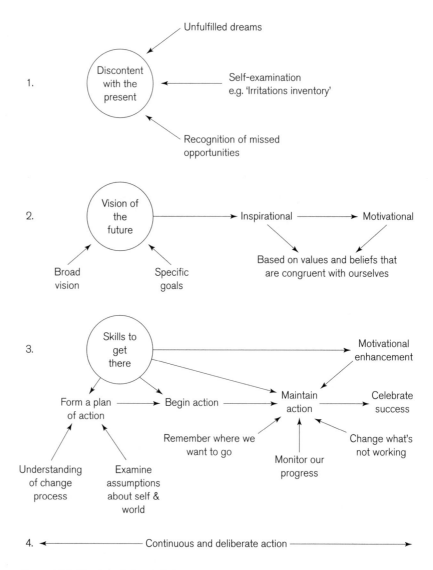

Figure 12.2 The foundations of change

How do we create change?

If we want to make real, lasting change we need to
make sure that all areas of our lives are supporting us
in reaching our goals. The House of Change reminds

us that we need to alter our thoughts, feelings and behaviour and set up the situation or our environment so that we are supported in making change. Changing just one of these four probably will not bring us the results we want, or at least the change won't work for very long.

The Coach Yourself programme

Step 1 An irritations inventory

Think about the main areas of your life. In each of these areas think about what it is that you are not enjoying. What are the things that make your life uncomfortable? What are those irritating things that you've learned to tolerate and put up with? Here's a list of ideas to get you started. Add your personal irritations if these don't match your life:

Working life	Work performance
Working for a lousy boss	Unmanageable e-mail and voice mail
Too stressed	Poor time management
Insufficient resources	Unclear job role
Insufficient pay	Not organized
Low work satisfaction	Poor relationship with work colleagues
Inadequate training and support	Over-long work hours
Working in the wrong occupation	Not delegating enough
Poor working conditions	No recognition / reward
Dysfunctional organization culture	Poor leadership skills
What else?	*What else?*

Family life

Deteriorating relationship with partner
Children too messy/noisy
Not seeing relatives
Not enough family time
Family life feels like a burden
Poor relationship with children
Lack of communication

What else?

Career development

No explicit written business/career plan
Fear of losing your job
Dead-end career path

What else?

Physical health

Overweight
Feeling unfit
Lack of energy
Unhealthy, unbalanced diet
Not enough exercise
Back/neck pain
Drug/alcohol intake
Smoking

What else?

Emotional life

Feeling too stressed or fearful
Feeling down or depressed
Sense of being lost
Being perfectionist
Unhappy with appearance
Poor time management
Lonely and isolated
Anxiety about the future

What else?

Money/finances

Unmanageable credit card bills
Unpaid bills keep piling up
Not enough provision for retirement
Not enough life/health insurance
Bank overdraft
Not enough money for lifestyle
Worry about money

What else?

Personal growth

Lack of intellectual stimulation
No spiritual direction
Poor self-acceptance
Sense of stagnation
No participation in the local community
Need to 'know more'
Lack of time for self-reflection

What else?

Home situation	Social life
Size, type of house/home	Socially isolated
Not your preferred residential area	Never going out for recreation
Home constantly too messy	Lack of fun in your life
Home needs redecorating	Friends who 'use' you
Car/appliances need repair or	Small social circle
replacement	Too many people in social life
Rent/mortgage repayments too high	Only superficial social contacts
Furniture needs replacing	Lack of meaningful friendships
Washing-up never done	

What else? *What else?*

Any other life areas or irritations not listed that are relevant to you?

What does the research show?

The idea that it is worthwhile spending time examining one's life goes back at least to Socrates – 'the unexamined life is not worth living'. But pyschological research also supports the process of self-assessment or self-examination in order to dismantle those irritating barriers to personal growth.

Often the nagative things that we learned to tolerate are in fact quite easy to identify and change. As far back as 1954, studies[6] found that systematically taking a personal inventory helped people reach their goals quicker, and in 1976 studies[7] found that self-assessment increased self-awareness and personal well-being. What's more, this process is effective for enhancing a wide range of life issues, including career development,[8] hyperactivity,[9] and sales performance.[10]

Step 2 Select an area to work on

From your irritations inventory or your previous experience select an area of your life in which you'd like to see some changes. You may of course choose more than one.

◆ Life area one is

◆ Life area two is

◆ Life area three is

Step 3 Understand change

Task: work out which stage you're at

James Prochaska and Carlo DiClemente's work on the stages of change shows that change is a complex, dynamic process which has six stages. For the life area(s) you choose to work on, identify the stage of change that you are at.

Stage of change	Explanation
Pre-contemplation	I haven't been thinking about making changes in this area and I don't intend to in the near future
Contemplation	I have thought about making changes in this area of my life, but haven't actually done anything about it yet.
Preparation	I am intending to (or have just started within the past week) to make some changes in this area of my life.
Action	I have been actively making real changes in this area of my life for at least the last month.
Maintenance	I have been actively making successful changes in this area for about six months.

Relapse	I had started to make real changes but I seem to have slipped back into my old ways.

Task: aim for the next stage

You need to be able to move yourself from contemplation, through to preparation and into action, and from action to maintenance and termination. Certain techniques work particularly well at specific stages.[11]

Stage of change	Tips to move forward
Pre-contemplation	Focus less on changing others, or demanding that the situation changes, and focus more on what you are doing to create or maintain the problem. Look to see what factors could support you in making change – friends, social networks, what you could change in your environment that would help you reach your goals.
Contemplation	Get angry about how the problem has had a negative impact on your life. Turn your attention from trying to understand the 'why' of the problem to the 'how' of the solution. Tune into the reasons for change rather than the reasons not to change. Examine a wide range of options.
Preparation	Don't rush into change – develop a sound action plan first. Make a genuine personal and public committment to change.

Action	Continue to see yourself from a new perspective – focus on the future and your new changed self.
	Focus on how good you'll feel when you make these changes.
	Continue to make a genuine personal and public commitment to change.
	Keep busy and focused on action and activity.
	Make sure your situation or environment continues to support you in making change.
	Find someone else to co-coach or help.
	Avoid complacency – avoid relapse.
	Reward yourself at regular intervals.
Maintenance	Recognize that maintenance is a long-term, ongoing process.
	Give something back to those who helped you, and help others make similar changes.
	Consolidate and build on the benefits of the action stage.
Relapse	Accept that relapse is normal.
	Learn from past mistakes.
	Abandon past failed 'solutions'.
	Move back into action as soon as possible.

Step 4 Creating dreams

Task: write yourself a letter from the future

Choose a date in the future – this should be at least three months' time, and up to one or two years. Imagine that you have travelled in time to this date and you are sitting down writing a letter to your coach (which is yourself) telling them how great your life is now, and how you've managed to get rid of so many of those things that were irritating you.

When you write this letter, rather than focusing on the negative – the things that you want to be rid of – write about what you would like to have happening – focus on the solution, not the mere absence of the problem. Don't forget to include the whole of the House of Change – situation, behaviour, thoughts, and feelings. Also write about how your needs and values are being met and expressed and how these are motivating you. You might like to use a separate piece of paper for your letter from the future.

This letter from the future is a simple and very powerful tool for change. Over the years I've consistently been amazed at the fabulous results people have achieved using this technique. When I started using this technique in my coaching practice I thought it would appeal only to individuals who saw themselves as being 'creative' types. But this technique has been used successfully by an incredibly wide range of personality types, including elite Royal Australian Air Force test pilots, captains of industry, school teachers, builders and construction workers, and accountants. It really works!

Task: identify your needs and values

Values and needs are powerful motivating factors in our lives, so much so that throughout history people have been prepared to die for them. On a less extreme basis, people who act in accord with their needs and values are more likely to achieve their goals. If you want to create real change in your life you must take time to identify the values and needs that are important to you.

You must make sure that these needs and values are really *your own personal needs and values*. We need to take time to examine this – time to make the implicit explicit. It is easy to unthinkingly take on other people's or society's values when deep down we know they are not our own. If in the past you have had difficulty in making changes, it may be that you have been trying to make changes based on what others want.

What does the research show?

In a study of 271 sales people, Michael Swenson[12] and Joel Herche found that individuals' values were predictive of sales performance – individuals whose work was in alignment with their core values had greater sales performance.

Here is a list of some values and needs that may be relevant to you. Read it and identify the needs and values that are important to you in each of the two or three areas of life you want to work on changing.

Accomplishment	Fun and enjoyment	Physical health
Acknowledgement	Freedom to choose	Power and authority
Adaptability	Friendship	Profit
Artistry	Helping society/others	Recognition
Authenticity	Honesty	Respect
Beauty and aesthetics	Humour	Security
Being admired	Independence	Self-determination
Being alone	Influencing others	Self-expression
Being different	Integrity	Self-fulfilment
Being valued	Intellectual stimulation	Sensuality
Being with others	Interaction with public	Sexuality
Belonging	Intimacy	Solitude
Change and variation	Joy	Spirituality
Collaboration	Love	Stability
Communication	Making decisions	Status
Community	Medium pace	Success
Competition	Meeting challenges	Support
Comradeship	Money	Time
Control over time	Order	Tranquillity
Creativity	Participation	Zest
Excitement	Peace	
Expanding knowledge	Personal empowerment	

What other values and needs are important to you that are not on this list?

Now write down up to seven needs and for each life area check whether these needs are met 'Always, Often, Sometimes, Seldom or Never'. Rank from 1 to 7 the relative importance you place on each need or value.

My needs and values are	Rank importance from 1 to 7	In this area of my life these are met				
		Always	Often	Sometimes	Seldom	Never

You need to make sure that your most important core needs and values are expressed and supported in your change programme.

Step 5 **Maximize your motivation**

Having clearly defined goals has been shown to be an effective way of bringing about successful change in your life. But goals need to be SMART.

Specific: vague goals lead to vague, half-hearted attempts to achieve them.

Measurable: we need to be able to evaluate our progress.

Attractive: if we don't want it, we're unlikely to put in a sustained effort.

Realistic: we must be capable of achieving the goal.

Time-framed: we need to have an appropriate time frame in mind.

Here's an example:

Life area physical health	
Project name 'The fit, flexible and pain-free me!'	
Sign/symbol photo of myself when younger looking, active and fit	
Purpose to reduce neck and back pain, to be fit, lose weight	
Values respect for my body, personal empowerment	
Goal	*Be fit and flexible, reduce neck and back pain*
Specific	*Swim 10 laps in 25m pool, 3 times a week*
Measurable	*Keep monitoring log on office wall*
Attractive	*Will feel fit, flexible, more productive*
Realistic	*Pool near work, can swim before work*
Time-framed	*Have weekly plan, start on Monday*

Life area	
Project name	
Sign/symbol	
Purpose	
Values	
Goal	
S pecific	
M easurable	
A ttractive	
R ealistic	
T ime-framed	

Rate how attractive this goal is   1 – 2 – 3 – 4 – 5 – 6 – 7 – 8 – 9 – 10

Rate how challenging this goal is   1 – 2 – 3 – 4 – 5 – 6 – 7 – 8 – 9 – 10

Rate your confidence in reaching your goal   1 – 2 – 3 – 4 – 5 – 6 – 7 – 8 – 9 – 10

Ideally, your scores will be in the following ranges:

  Attractiveness 8 – 10   Challenge 7 – 9   Confidence 7 – 9

If your scores fall outside these ranges you may need to rework your plans by making them more/less attractive/challenging.

Any changes?

Task: weigh up the positive and negative effects of making a change

To stay motivated you need to think about the positive effects of making a change and the negative effects of failing to do so.

Write down the positive and negative impacts of making changes in each of your chosen life area(s).

Negative effects which will be caused by my failure to make changes in life area 1	Positive effects in my life when I do make changes in life area 1

Ask yourself … which side looks better to you?

Step 6 Turn Your ANTs into PETs!

What kind of negative self-talk (automatic negative thoughts) is likely to come up as you begin to work on your change project?

Ask yourself: 'How would thinking like this affect me? Will it help or hinder my progress?'

If you decide that this kind of thinking will not enhance your performance, ask yourself: 'What kind of positive self-talk (PETS – performance-enhancing thoughts) would be useful?' Write down these ideas and keep them where you can see them.

You might like to take an inventory using a table like the one below.

Event	ANTs	Feelings	Evaluate ANTs *How are they inaccurate?* *how are they unhelpful?*	New PETs

Step 7 Focus on the solution

Task: build up your motivation to change by spending some time thinking about your new life. See it in your mind's eye. Run through it like a movie – what's happening in this positive, solution-focused future life? Allow yourself to enjoy a day-dream about the future.

◆ What's the *situation* like? How is it different and better than the past?

◆ What are you doing? How is your *behaviour* different and more effective than the past?

◆ What are you *thinking*? How do these new positive, solution-focused thoughts enhance your life?

◆ How do you *feel*? How do these feelings support you in reaching your goals?

For each life area you choose, ask yourself the following questions.

How would I notice if I reached my goal?

What would be different about the situation or environment?

How would I be behaving, talking, feeling?

How would other people notice that I'd changed?

Task: write out how your thoughts, feelings, behaviour and the situation will be supporting you in reaching your goals. We're also interested in how the interaction between our thoughts, feelings and behaviours help us reach our goals. Use the House of Change as a guiding template and think about the following questions:

◆ What is your goal?

◆ How does the situation support you in reaching your goal?

◆ What small changes can you make in your usual environment that will help you reach your goal?

- What are you doing (behaviour) that helps you reach your goal?

- What are you thinking and how does that impact on your feelings and behaviour?

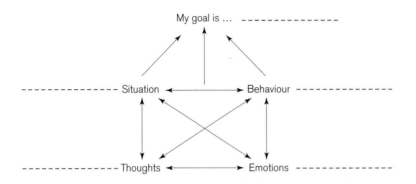

Task: check and see how far you've progressed already!

In solution-focused coaching we often find that people have already moved a considerable way towards the realization of their goals even before they start systematically working on achieving them. Take a moment to rate how much progress you've already made.

0	1	2	3	4	5	6	7	8	9	10
No Change				Moderate goal achievement				Complete goal achievement		

Step 8 Gather your resources

Task: choose a name for your project, and a symbol or sign to represent the project

Think about the development of your future life as a *project* you're going to undertake. Making this project as real as possible can be helpful in forwarding the action. So, choose a name for your project and a sign or symbol to represent the project. The sign or symbol can be anything you like, as long as it has meaning for you.

Having an easily accessible mental image of the project helps you to stay on track. For this sign or symbol you might want to do a sketch, or collect some item or memento and put it where you can't fail to see it.

Task: map your resources

What resources do you have that will help you in moving towards your goals?

◆ physical resources

◆ mental/intellectual resources

◆ emotional resources

◆ spiritual resources

◆ financial resources

◆ situational resources.

Task: think about your life areas and the things you want to achieve. Look back in time to where you have faced similar situations and challenges. What strengths did you have that helped you deal with the situation? Note that it doesn't matter if you were 'successful' or not. What matters is that you recognize that you really do have the abilities to succeed. Make a note of at least five strengths that you bring with you to your life challenges.

Challenges   **Strengths**

Step 9 **Staying on track**

Task: develop an action plan

Small steps lead to big gains. When developing an action plan, remember: **K**eep **I**t **S**imple.

Ask yourself: what would be a small but significant step that would move me towards my future?

What would be the next step after that one? And the next one? And the next one? Develop a series of small steps that will make your project really happen. Describe these steps in ways that outline what you will *actually be doing*. This way you have an easy-to-follow plan of action. For example:

If your goal is to make your work more *enjoyable*:

You could write:

'I will focus on the things that I enjoy in my work. I will keep a note in a journal of the enjoyable things (however small) that happen at work and I will find a way to make these things happen more often.'

If your goal is to make your work more *productive*:

You could write:

'I will take note of the times when I am productive, work out what I am doing well at those times and do more of that. I will examine my time management and improve on it. I will keep a log of my time use for one week, analyze where I am wasting time, and make moves to reduce these time-wasters. If necessary I will seek out a mentor to help me improve my time-management skills.'

If your goal is to make your work more *harmonious*:

You could write:

'I will focus on other people's good points. I will talk enthusiastically about my work. In my interactions with others I will listen to what they have to say before responding. I will express my views in a moderate fashion and develop empathy for other people. I will acknowledge others' successes. I will not fuel heated conversations; rather, I will be a voice of calm, reason and moderation.'

For each of the life areas you want to work on, plan a series of small steps:

◆ Step 1

◆ Step 2

◆ Step 3

◆ Step 4

◆ Step 5

Make more than five steps if you like.

Task: anticipate problems and work out how to solve them

Ask yourself:

◆ What obstacles might slow down my progress?

◆ What setbacks might occur?

◆ How can I overcome these obstacles and prepare for any setbacks?

Make a note of the factors working for and against change.

Task: optimize your optimism

List five reasons why you will be successful:
1
2
3
4
5

Task: commit to action and make a decision to begin

Now we need to commit to action – thinking, wishing, wanting are not enough, we need to DO IT and to start RIGHT NOW! Now that you know how much you have to gain, ask yourself: 'Am I prepared to give it a real go?' Put it in writing.

My Contract For Change

I .... take personal responsibility for creating change in my life. I will begin the project called .... and formally make a contract with myself to see this project through. I've listed the benefits of living in the solution and I am going to start living in the solution from ....

Signed ....
Date ....
Witness ....

What does the research show?

Making a written contact to make changes really helps people stick to their change committment. In one study[13] schoolchildren aged 9 to 12 made a written contract to study consistently. They spent more time studying and their grades increased significantly. Making a written contract helps people stick to exercise programmes[14] and helps maintain motivation when looking for a new job following long-term unemployment.[15] Written contracting has also been used extensively and successfully in suicide prevention.[16]

We now have many of the skills we need to create real change. We understand the change process, have looked at our values and needs, and learned how to align our thoughts, feelings and behaviour with our goals. We know the value of structuring the situation or environment to support us in reaching our goals and we've set SMART goals, formed a plan of action and made a written committment to change.

Now we need to set up a system that will keep us on track. We need to be able to regularly monitor and evaluate our progress and do more of what works, and less of what doesn't work. This kind of feedback is vital if we are going to make real change (*see* Figure 12.3).

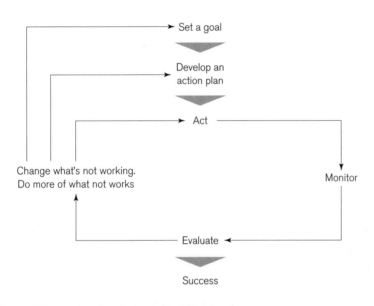

Figure 12.3 A system for staying on track for change

Task: monitor your progress

In order to monitor your progress and evaluate how your project is going, you will need to keep a journal of your project. What kind of journal format will be best for you? Will you need a folder to put your notes in? Is a diary best? What other journal-type processes might be useful?

Here's an example of one kind of simple weekly self-monitoring log that you can use to keep a record of the actions you need to take In order to create your desired changes.

	Change Action 1 Done Yes/No	Change Action 2 Done Yes/No
Monday		
Tuesday		
Wednesday		
Thursday		
Friday		
Saturday		
Sunday		

Each week, preferably at the same time on the same day, set aside some time to hold a self-coaching session. This need take only ten minutes, but it will significantly enhance your probability of success.

What does the research show?

Regularly spending a short time elevating how you are sticking to a change programme increases your chance of successful change. It has even been found[17] that regularly examining household energy use on a bi-weekly basis reduces energy consumption. Regular self-assessment has also helped overly aggressive baseball coaches to develop more effective coaching behaviour and heightened self-awareness.[18]

Task: use the GROW self-coaching method

Use the GROW model to monitor your progress.

In your diary, schedule a weekly GROW session. Take time to look at:

◆ **GOALS**

◆ **REALITY**

◆ **OPTIONS**

◆ **WRAP-UP** (the way forward – *see* Chapter 9).

Step 10 Getting help

You can't get support unless you let people know what you're doing and why you're going to be successful. So, let people know that you are starting this project – broadcast your good news! Who will you share your news with?

Does anyone need to know about your plan?

Sometimes, for example in business, we need to inform others of our plans. In other situations it is best not to tell people but to just get on with it. A simple rule of thumb is to share your 'up' goals only with those who will support you in attaining them. For example, if you want to be the best salesperson in your company, share that goal only with your sales manager, not the salespeople you are in competition with.

Co-coaching

Making change is often easier with a co-coach.

Who can you co-coach in making changes?

What kind of guidelines will you need? How will you co-coach – do you prefer to co-coach by phone or face to face?

Put something back – give back to others

What can you do in order to give a bit back? How can you help other people who are also trying to make changes?

Step 11 Celebrate your success

How can you celebrate on a daily basis and at the end of your project?

You might like to develop a success-monitoring log in which you keep a note of your success and the feelings associated with each success. Focusing on positive outcomes in a monitoring log is a powerful means of keeping the action plan moving forward.

	Successes I had today and how I felt
Monday	
Tuesday	
Wednesday	
Thursday	
Friday	
Saturday	
Sunday	

Step 12 Draw up an action plan for the first four weeks of your change programme

What needs to be done, and when? Draw up or use a time planner like this one below and put it up where you can see it. Remember to renew this when the four weeks are up.

Monday	Tuesday	Wednesday	Thursday	Friday	Saturday	Sunday
Monday	Tuesday	Wednesday	Thursday	Friday	Saturday	Sunday
Monday	Tuesday	Wednesday	Thursday	Friday	Saturday	Sunday
Monday	Tuesday	Wednesday	Thursday	Friday	Saturday	Sunday

Now draw up a detailed plan for the following week. Set yourself a goal
to achieve each day. Work out below what you are going to do each day.
You might like to rate your successes in achieving your goals on a daily
basis on a scale from 1 to 10.

Day	Things to be done and things I did	Success rating 1 to 10
Monday		
Tuesday		
Wednesday		
Thursday		
Friday		
Saturday		
Sunday		

**You MUST do something each day that moves you
towards your goal.**

If your plan doesn't call for concrete action each day, work out how you can strengthen your commitment on a daily basis.

You could work on developing your vision — write about it, collect newspaper clippings, magazine pictures, do some research/reading. Whatever you do, you *must* keep a record of it.

Finally, ask yourself: How will I feel if I make this plan and *DON'T* carry it out?

Circle one of the following

Absolutely   Really bad   OK   Pretty good   Fantastic!
terrible

How intensely will you feel this?
Check one number below

1   2   3   4   5   6   7   8   9   10

How will you feel if you *DO* stick to your plan?
Circle one of the following

Absolutely   Really bad   OK   Pretty good   Fantastic!
terrible

How intensely will you feel this?
Check one number below

1   2   3   4   5   6   7   8   9   10

Ask yourself: which feeling would you rather have?
It's your choice!

It's your life — what are you going to do with it?

further reading

Chapter 1

1   di Lampedusa, G.C. (1960) *The Leopard*, London, Collins Harville.

2   Ridderstrale, J. and Nordstrom, K. (1999) *Funky Business*, London, Book House Publishing.

Chapter 2

1   'Coaching can be a good things for organizations and employees alike', (2000) *Training and Development*, Feb.

2   'Corporate coaching growing as retention tool' (1999) *HR Focus*, Oct.

3   Bartlett, C.A. and Ghoshal, S. (1995) 'Changing the role of top management – beyond systems to people', *Harvard Business Review*, 73 (3), 132–42, May–June.

Chapter 3

1   Bridges, W. (1986) 'Managing organizational transitions', *Organizational Dynamics*, 15 (1), 24–33.

2   Prochaska, J.O., Norcross, J.C. and DiClemente, C.C. (1994) *Changing For Good*, New York, Avon Books.

3   Prochaska, J.O., Velicier, W.F, Rossie, J.S. and Goldsten, M.G. (1994) 'Stages of change and decisional balance for 12 problem behaviors', *Health Psychology*, 13 (1), 39–46.

4   Lan, W.Y., Bradley, L. and Parr, G. (1993) 'The effects of a self-monitoring process on college students' learning in an introductory statisstics course', *Journal of Experimental Education*, 62 (1), 26–40.

5   DeNisi, A.S., Robbins, T.L. and Summers, T.P. (1997) 'Organization, processing, and use of performance information: a cognitive role for appraisal instruments', *Journal of Applied Social Psychology*, 27 (21), 1884–1905.

6   Rossi, J.S., Prochaska, J.O. and DiClemente, C.C. (1988) 'Processes of change in heavy and light smokers', *Journal of Substance Abuse*, 1 (1), 1–9.

7   Head, S. and Brookhart, A. (1997) 'Lifestyle modification and relapse-prevention training during treatment for weight loss', *Behavior Therapy*, 28 (2), 307–21.

8   Gollwitzer, P.M., Heckhausen, H. and Ratajczak, H. (1990) 'From weighing to willing: approaching a change decision through pre- or postdecisional mentation', *Organizational Behavior & Human Decision Processes*, 45 (1), 41–65.

9   Renata Adler in Stein, M. (ed.) (1993) *The Wit and Wisdom of Woman*.

Chapter 4

1   Bellanti, A. (1997) 'Hypnosis for weight loss: a case history', *Australian Journal of Clinical Hypnotherapy & Hypnosis*, 18 (2), 55–9.

2   Stanton, H.E. (1978) 'A one-session hypnotic approach to modifying smoking behavior', *International Journal of Clinical & Experimental Hypnosis*, 26 (1), 22–9.

3   Buñel, Luis (1985) *My Last Breath*, London, Fontana Paperbacks.

4   Furman, Ben and Ahola, Tapani (1992) *Solution Talk: Hosting Therapeutic Conversations*, New York, Norton & Co.

5   Lavy, E.H., Van den Hout, M. and Arntz, A. (1993) 'Attentional bias and spider phobia: conceptual and clinical issues', *Behaviour Research & Therapy*, 31 (1), 17–24.

6   Martinez-Pons, M. (1997) 'The relation of emotinal intelligence with selected areas of personal functioning', *Imagination, Cognition & Personality*, 17 (1), 3–13.

7   Kuiper, N.A. and Dance, K.A. (1994) 'Dysfunctional attitudes, roles, stress evaluations, and psychological well-being', *Journal of Research in Personality*, 28 (2), 245–62.

8   Francis, M.E. and Pennebaker, J.W. (1992) 'Putting stress into words: the impact of writing on physiological, absentee, and self-reported emotional well-being measures', *American Journal of Health Promotion*, 6 (4), 280–87.

9   Ridderstrale, J. and Nordstrom, K. (1999) *Funky Business*, London, Book House Publishing.

Chapter 5

1   Druckman, D and Bjork, R.A. (1991) *In the Mind's Eye: Enhancing Human Performance*, Washington DC, National Academy Press.

2 Butt, D.S. (1987) *The Psychology of Sport: The Behavior, Motivation, Personality and Performance of Athletes*, New York, Van Nostrand Reinhold Co, Inc.

3 *New Scientist*, 4 April 1998.

4 Jackson, Susan A. and Csikszentmihalyi, M. (1999) *Flow in Sports*, Human Kinetics.

5 Locke, E.A. (1996) 'Motivation through conscious goal setting', *Applied & Preventive Psychology*, 5 (2), 117–24.

6 Harriott, J. and Ferrari, J.R. (1996) 'Prevalence of procrastination among samples of adults', *Psychological Reports*, 78 (2), 611–16.

7 Sapadin, L. and Maguire, J. (1996) *It's About Time!*, New York, Penguin.

8 Sarmiento, R.F. (1993) *Reality Check: Twenty Questions to Screw Your Head on Straight*, Huston, Bunker Hill Press.

Chapter 6

1 Ellis, A. and Harper, R.A. (1961) *A New Guide to Rational Living*, Englewood Cliffs, N.J., Prentice Hall.

2 Ellis, A. and Harper, R.A. (1961) *A New Guide to Rational Living*, Englewood Cliffs, N.J., Prentice Hall.

3 Thompson, S.C. (1999) 'Illusions of control: how we overestimate our personal influence', *Current Directions in Psychological Science*, 8 (6), 187–90.

4 Zak, A., Hunton, L., Kuhn, R. and Parks, J. (1997), 'Effects of need for control on personal relationships', *Journal of Social Psychology*, 137 (5), 671–2.

5 Kets de Vries, M.F.R. and Miller, D. (1991) 'Leadership styles and organizational cultues: the shaping of neurotic organizations' in M.F.R. Kets de Vries and D. Miller (eds) *Organizations on the Couch: Clinical Perspectives on Organizational Behavior and Change*, The Jossey-Bass Management Series, San Francisco, Jossey-Bass.

6 MacKay, M. and Fanning, P. (1997) *Prisoners of Belief: Exposing and Changing Beliefs that Control Your Life*, New Harbinger.

7 Beck, A., Rush, A., Shaw, B and Emery, G. (1979) *Cognitive Therapy of Depression*, New York, Guilford Press.

8 Wells, A. (1997) *Cognitive Therapy of Anxiety Disorders*, New York, John Wiley.

9 Green, D. (1983) 'A cognitive approach to examination anxiety', *British Journal of Cognitive Psychotherapy*, 1 (2), 24–32.

10 Bernard, M.E. and DiGiuseppe, R. (1994) *Rational-Emotive Consultation in Applied Settings*, pp. x, 210, Hillsdale, N.J., Lawrence Erlbaum Associates, Inc.

11 Hattie, J., Biggs, J. and Purdie, N. (1996) 'Effects of learning skills interventions on student learning: a meta-analysis', *Review of Educational Research*, 66 (2), 99–136.

Chapter 7

1   De Shazer, S. (1994) *Words Were Originally Magic*, New York, Norton & Co.

2   Osenton, T. and Chang, J. (1999) 'Solution-oriented classroom management: a proactive application with young children', *Journal of Systemic Therapies*, 18 (2), 65–76.

3   Corcoran, J. and Stephenson, M. (2000) 'The effectiveness of solution-focused therapy with child behavior problems: a preliminary report', *Families in Society*, 81, 468–74.

4   Mason, W.H., Chandler, M.C. and Grasso, B.C. (1995) 'Solution based techniques applied to addictions: a clinics experience in shifting paradigms', *Alcoholism Treatment Quarterly*, 13 (4), 39–49.

5   Quicke, J. and Winter, C. (1994) 'Labelling and learning: an interactionist perspective,' *Support for Learning*, 9 (1), 16–21.

6   Gingrich, W.J. and Eisengart, S. (1999). Paper prepared for presentation to the International Family Therapy Association, Akron, Ohio, April 15.

7   De Shazer, S., and Lipchik, E. (1984) 'Frames and reframing', *Family Therapy Collections*, 11, 88–97.

8   Bayliss, T. (1999) *Clock This*, London, Headline.

Chapter 8

1   Buzan, T. (1994) *The Mind Map Book: How to Use Radiant Thinking to Maximize your Brain's Untapped Potential*, New York, Dutton.

2   Kabat-Zinn, J., Massion, A.O., Kristeller, J. and Peterson, L.G. (1992) 'Effectiveness of a meditation-based stress reduction program in the treatment of anxiety disorders', *American Journal of Psychiatry*, 149 (7), 936–43.

3   Shapiro, S.L, Schwartz, G.E. and Bonner, G. (1998) 'Effects of mindfulness-based stress reduction on medical and premedical students', *Journal of Behavioral Medicine*, 21 (6), 581–99.

4   Baldwin, M.A. (2001) 'Relational schema activation: does Bob Zajonc ever scowl at you from the back of your mind?' *Unraveling the*

Complexities of Social Life: A Festschrift in Honor of Robert B. Zajonc, pp. 55–67, Washington, DC, American Psychological Association.

5   Brewer, W.F. (2000) 'Bartlett, functionalism, and modern schema theories', *Journal of Mind & Behavior*, 21 (1–2), 37–44.

6   Eskritt, M. (1999) 'The influence of symbolic notation on memory in adults and children', *Dissertation Abstracts International: Section B: the Sciences & Engineering*, 59 (10–B), 5597.

7   Macklin, M.C. (1996) 'Preschoolers' learning of brand names from visual cues', *Journal of Consumer Research*, 23 (3), 251–61.

8   Thoreson, R.W. and Budd, F.C. (1987) 'Self-help groups and other group procedures for treating alcohol problems, *Treatment and Prevention of Alcohol Problems: A Resource Manual. Personality, Psychopathology, and Pyschotherapy*, Orlando, FL, Academic Press.

Chapter 9

1   Wylie, A.M. (1986) 'Ratio strain: conditions of performance decrement of human operant behavior', *Dissertation Abstracts International*, 47 (2–B), 828.

2   Buñuel, Luis (1985) *My Last Breath*, Fontana Paperbacks.

3   Whitmore, J. (1996) *Coaching for Performance*, 2nd edn, London, Nicholas Brealey.

4   Febbraro, G.A.R. and Clum, G.A. (1998) 'Meta-analytic investigation of the effectiveness of self-regulatory components in the treatment of adult problem behaviors', *Clinical Psychology Review*, 18 (2), 143–61.

5   Johnston-O'Connor, E.J. and Kirschenbaum, D.S. (1986) 'Something succeeds like success: positive self-monitoring for unskilled golfers', *Cognitive Therapy & Research*, 10 (1), 123–36.

6   St Lawrence, J.S., McGrath, M.L., Oakley, M.E. and Sult, S.C. (1983) 'Stress management training for law students: cognitive-behavioral intervention', *Behavioral Sciences & the Law*, 1 (4), 101–10.

Chapter 10

1   Ballard, J.G. (1994) *Empire of the Sun*, London, Flamingo.

2   Scandura, T.A. (1992) 'Mentorship and career mobility: an empirical investigation', *Journal of Organizational Behavior*, 13 (2), 169–74.

3   Kohler, F.W., Ezell, H.K. and Paluselli, M. (1999) 'Promoting changes in teachers' conduct of student pair activities: an examination of reciprocal peer coaching', *Journal of Special Education*, 33 (3), 154–65.

4   Scarnati, J.T., Kent, W. and MacKenzie, W. (1993) 'Peer coaching and cooperative learning: one room school concept', *Journal of Instructional Psychology*, 20 (1), 65–71.

5   Whitworth, L., Kimsey-House, H. and Sandahl, P. (1998) *Co-active Coaching: New Skills for Coaching People towards Success in Work and Life*, Palo Alto, CA, Davies-Black.

Chapter 11

1   Anderson, D.W. (2000) 'Personality, self-efficacy and managerial leadership behaviour', *Dissertation Abstracts International: Section B: the Sciences & Engineering*, 60 (9–B).

2   Craske, M.G. and Craig, K.D. (1984) 'Musical performance anxiety: the three-systems model and self-efficacy theory', *Behaviour Research & Therapy*, 22 (3), 267–80.

3   Thomas, J.M. (1999) 'Relationship efficacy: the prediction of goal attainment by dating couples', *Dissertation Abstracts International: Section B: the Sciences & Engineering*, 59.

4   Wurtele, S.K. (1986) 'Self-efficacy and athletic performance: a review', *Journal of Social & Clinical Psychology*, 4 290–301.

5   Lee, C. (1984) 'Efficacy expectations and outcome expectations as predictors of performance in a snake-handling task', *Cognitive Therapy & Research*, 8 (5), 509–16.

6   Seligman, M.E.P. (1991) *Learned Optimism*, Sydney, Random House.

7   Mullis, R.J. (1992) 'Measures of economic well-being as predictors of psychological well-being', *Social Indicators Research*, 26 (2), 119–35.

8   Furnham, A. and Cheng, H. (1999) 'Personality as predictor of mental health and happiness in the East and West', *Personality & Individual Differences*, 27 (3), 395–403.

Chapter 12

1   Burns, D.D. and Auerbach, A.H. (1992) 'Does homework compliance enhance receovery from depression? *Psychiatric Annals*, 22 (9), 464–9.

2   Westling, B.E. and Ost, L.-G. (1999) 'Brief cognitive behaviour therapy of panic disorder', *Scandinavian Journal of Behaviour Therapy*, 28 (2), 49–57.

3   Van der Ploeg, H.M. and Van der Ploeg-Stapert, J.D. (1986) 'A multifaceted behavioral group treatment for test anxiety', *Psychological Reports*, 58 (2), 535–42.

4   Moffett, L.A. and Stoklosa, J.M. (1976) 'Group therapy for socially anxious and unassertive young veterans', *International Journal of Group Psychotherapy*, 26 (4), 421–30.

5 Burns, D.D. and Spangler, D.L. (2000) 'Does psychotherapy homework lead to improvements in depression in cognitive-behavioral therapy or does improvement lead to increased homework compliance?', *Journal of Consulting & Clinical Psychology*, 68 (1), 46–56.

6 Sandler, J. (1954) 'Studies in psychopathology using a self-assessment inventory', *British Journal of Medical Psychology*, 27, 142–5.

7 Dana, R.H. and Fitzgerald, J. (1976) 'Educational self-assessment: a course-in-oneself', *College Student Journal*, 10 (4), 317–23.

8 Niles, S.G. and Usher, C.H. (1993) 'Applying the career-development assessment and counselling model to the case of Rosie', *Career Development Quarterly*, 42 (1), 61–66.

9 Wiggins, D., Singh, K., Getz, H.G. and Hutchins, D.E. (1999) 'Effects of brief group intervention for adults with attention deficit/hyperactivity disorder', *Journal of Mental Health Counselling*, 21 (1), 82–92.

10 McIntyre, R.P., Claxton, R.P., Anselmi, K. and Wheatley, E.E. (2000) 'Cognitive style as an antecedent to adaptiveness, customer orientation, and self-perceived selling performance', *Journal of Business & Psychology*, 15 (2), 259–70.

11 Prochaska, J.O., Norcross, J.C. and DiClemente, C.C. (1994) *Changing For Good*, New York, Avon Books.

12 Swenson, M.J. and Herche, J. (1994) 'Social values and salesperson performance: an empirical examination', *Journal of the Academy of Marketing Science*, 22 (3), 283–9.

13 Beidel, D.C., Turner, S.M. and Taylor-Ferreira, J.C. (1999) 'Teaching study skills and test-taking strategies to elementary school students: the Testbusters program', *Behavior Modification*, 23 (4), 630–46.

14 Neale, A.V., Singleton, S.P., Dupuis, M.H. and Hess, J.W. (1990) 'The use of behavioral contracting to increase exercise activity', *American Journal of Health Promotion*, 4 (6), 441–7.

15 Leung, P. (1974) 'The use of behavior contracts in employability development planning, *Journal of Employment Counceling*, 11 (4), 150–53.

16 Stanford, E.J., Goetz, R.R. and Bloom, J.D. (1994) 'The No Harm Contract in the emergency assessment of suicidal risk', *Journal of Clinical Psychiatry*, 55 (8), 344–8.

17 De Boer, J. and Ester, P. (1985) 'The influence on behavior through information and feedback', *Nederlands Tijdschrift voor de Psychologie en Haar Grensgebieden*, 40 (2), 87–95.

18 De Marco, G.M.P., Jr., Mancini, V.H. and West, D.A. (1997) 'Reflections on change: a qualitative and quantitative analysis of a baseball coach's behavior', *Journal of Sport Behavior*, 20 (2), 135–63.